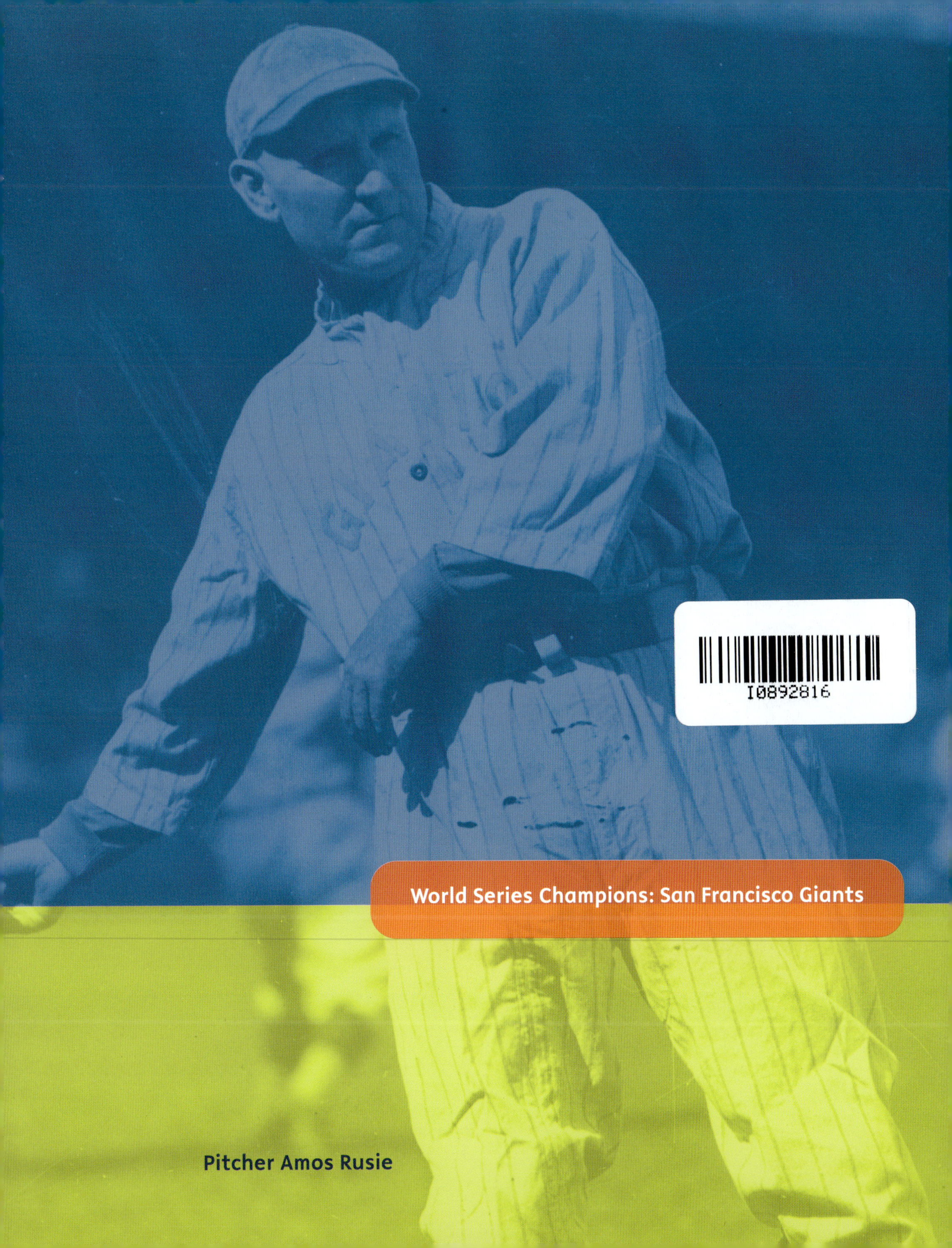

World Series Champions: San Francisco Giants

Pitcher Amos Rusie

Outfielder Barry Bonds

WORLD SERIES CHAMPIONS

SAN FRANCISCO GIANTS

MEGAN COOLEY PETERSON

CREATIVE EDUCATION / CREATIVE PAPERBACKS

Published by Creative Education and Creative Paperbacks
P.O. Box 227, Mankato, Minnesota 56002
Creative Education and Creative Paperbacks are imprints of
The Creative Company
www.thecreativecompany.us

Art Direction by Tom Morgan
Book production by Ciara Beitlich
Edited by Joe Tischler

Photographs by AP Images (David J. Griffin/Icon Sportswire), Corbis (Library of Congress, Robert Riger, Don Smith), Getty (Focus on Sport, Thearon W. Henderson, Brad Mangin, Sacramento Bee, Jamie Squire, Sarah Stier, Transcendental Graphics), iStock (muddymari)

Library of Congress Cataloging-in-Publication Data
Names: Peterson, Megan Cooley, author.
Title: San Francisco Giants / Megan Cooley Peterson.
Description: Mankato, MN : Creative Education and Creative Paperbacks, 2024. | Series: Creative sports. World Series champions | Includes index. | Audience: Ages 7-10 | Audience: Grades 2-3 | Summary: "Elementary-level text and engaging sports photos highlight the San Francisco Giants' MLB World Series wins and losses, plus sensational players associated with the professional baseball team such as Barry Bonds."-- Provided by publisher.
Identifiers: LCCN 2023008205 (print) | LCCN 2023008206 (ebook) | ISBN 9781640268340 (library binding) | ISBN 9781682773840 (paperback) | ISBN 9781640269873 (pdf)
Subjects: LCSH: San Francisco Giants (Baseball team)--History--Juvenile literature. | World Series (Baseball)--History--Juvenile literature.
Classification: LCC GV875.S34 P53 2024 (print) | LCC GV875.S34 (ebook) | DDC 796.357/640979461--dc23/eng/20230330
LC record available at https://lccn.loc.gov/2023008205
LC ebook record available at https://lccn.loc.gov/2023008206

Printed in China

2014 World Series Champions

Pitcher Tim Lincecum

CONTENTS

Home of the Giants

San Francisco is a hilly city in northern California. It is known for the famous Golden Gate Bridge. The city is also home to the Giants baseball team. The Giants have played at a **stadium** called Oracle Park since 2000.

The San Francisco Giants are a Major League Baseball (MLB) team. The Giants play in the National League (NL) West Division. Their **rivals** are the Los Angeles Dodgers. All teams try to win the World Series to become champions. The Giants have won it eight times!

Pitcher Christy Mathewson

Naming the Giants

The Giants started playing as the New York Gothams. In 1885, the team had a huge win. Manager Jim Mutrie was proud of his team. He called them "My big fellows! My giants!" A sportswriter started calling them the Giants. The name stuck.

Second baseman Larry Doyle

Giants History

The Giants played in their first World Series in 1905. They beat the Philadelphia Athletics. Over the next 19 years, the Giants reached eight World Series. Pitcher Christy Mathewson struck out batters. Larry Doyle drove in runs. The Giants won the **title** in 1921 and 1922. They beat the New York Yankees both times.

The Giants added two more World Series titles in New York. Then, in 1958, the team moved to San Francisco. Fans loved them. The Giants reached the World Series in 1962, 1989, and 2002. But they lost every time.

The Giants won their first championship in San Francisco in 2010. They beat the Texas Rangers. Catcher Buster Posey's strong hitting and arm helped his team win. Two years later, Posey and the Giants won again.

Catcher Buster Posey

Pitcher Madison Bumgarner

The Giants beat the Kansas City Royals in the 2014 World Series. Madison Bumgarner pitched a **shutout** in Game 5. It was the third championship for the Giants in five years!

Other Giants Stars

Many star pitchers have worn a Giants uniform. Amos Rusie won 234 games for the team in the 1890s. Tim Lincecum won two Cy Young Awards. The best pitchers receive it.

In 1951, Willie Mays joined the Giants. His big hits and amazing catches in center field made him a star. Outfielder Barry Bonds set a major-league record for **career** home runs.

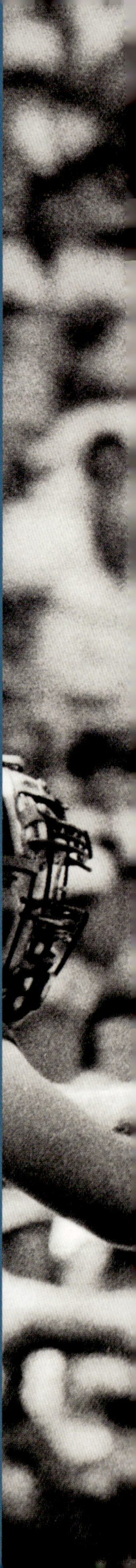

Outfielder Willie Mays

Shortstop Brandon Crawford

Newer players are hungry for more wins. Shortstop Brandon Crawford has earned four Gold Gloves and a Silver Slugger. The best fielders and hitters win these awards. Outfielder Joc Pederson smashed 23 homers in 2022. Pitcher Ross Stripling and fielder Mitch Haniger joined the team in 2023. Fans hope these All-Stars will bring another championship to San Francisco.

About the Giants

Started playing: 1883

League/division: National League, West Division

Team colors: black, orange, and white

Home stadium: Oracle Park

WORLD SERIES CHAMPIONSHIPS:

1905, 4 games to 1 over Philadelphia Athletics

1921, 5 games to 3 over New York Yankees

1922, 4 games to 0 over New York Yankees

1933, 4 games to 1 over Washington Senators

1954, 4 games to 0 over Cleveland Indians

2010, 4 games to 1 over Texas Rangers

2012, 4 games to 0 over Detroit Tigers

2014, 4 games to 3 over Kansas City Royals

San Francisco Giants website:
www.mlb.com/giants

Glossary

career—all the years a person spends doing a certain job

rival—a team that plays extra hard against another team

shutout—a game where one team doesn't score

stadium—a building with tiers of seats for spectators

title—another word for championship

Pitcher Ross Stripling

Index

1979 World Series Champions

Outfielder Andrew McCutchen

CONTENTS

Home of the Pirates

Pittsburgh, Pennsylvania, is nicknamed the "City of Bridges." It has nearly 450 of them! One of those bridges runs by a **stadium** called PNC Park. That's where the Pirates play baseball.

The Pittsburgh Pirates are a Major League Baseball (MLB) team. They compete in the National League (NL) Central Division. Their **rivals** are the Cincinnati Reds. All MLB teams want to win the World Series and become champions. The Pirates have done so five times!

Outfielder Kiki Cuyler

Naming the Pirates

The Pittsburgh club began in 1882. It was known as the Alleghenys. Prior to the 1891 season, Pittsburgh signed a player away from another team. The move was seen as "piratical," or piratelike. The team's name changed to "Pirates."

Shortstop Honus Wagner

Pirates History

Pittsburgh first played in the American Association. They moved to the NL in 1887. For many years, they weren't very good. That changed in 1900 when shortstop Honus Wagner joined the team. Wagner led the NL in batting average eight times. The Pirates won their first NL **pennant** in 1901. They played in the first World Series in 1903. But they lost. The Pirates were back in 1909, and this time they grabbed the win! They beat the Detroit Tigers in seven games.

The Pirates won their second **title** in 1925. Speedy outfielder Kiki Cuyler led the league in runs and triples. The team reached the World Series again two years later. But they were swept by the New York Yankees.

The Pirates fell into a **slump** that lasted more than 30 years. They didn't return to the World Series until 1960. They faced the Yankees again. Bill Mazeroski hit a game-winning home run in Game 7. This marked the Pirates' third championship.

Second baseman Bill Mazeroski

Outfielder Roberto Clemente

Pittsburgh was a fierce team in the 1970s. They reached the **playoffs** 6 times in 10 years. They won the World Series twice, beating the Baltimore Orioles in 1971 and 1979. Both wins were in seven games. Outfielder Roberto Clemente was great with his bat and glove. He led the NL in batting average 4 times and won 12 Gold Glove Awards. The best fielders in the league win that award.

Other Pirates Stars

Many stars have played for the Pirates. Willie Stargell hit nearly 500 home runs in 21 years. Outfielder Barry Bonds won two NL Most Valuable Player (MVP) Awards with the team. Outfielder Andrew McCutchen also won an MVP.

Outfielder/First baseman Willie Stargell

Third baseman Ke'Bryan Hayes

Third baseman Ke'Bryan Hayes is a hungry, rising star. So is pitcher David Bednar. Pirates fans hope they can help bring another championship home soon!

About the Pirates

Started playing: 1882

League/division: National League, Central Division

Team colors: black and gold

Home stadium: PNC Park

WORLD SERIES CHAMPIONSHIPS:

1909, 4 games to 3 over Detroit Tigers

1925, 4 games to 3 over Washington Senators

1960, 4 games to 3 over New York Yankees

1971, 4 games to 3 over Baltimore Orioles

1979, 4 games to 3 over Baltimore Orioles

Pittsburgh Pirates website:
www.mlb.com/pirates

Glossary

pennant—a league championship; a team that wins a pennant gets to play in the World Series

playoffs—games that the best teams play after a regular season to see who the champion will be

rival—a team that plays extra hard against another team

slump—a period of time when a team loses more games than it wins

stadium—a building with tiers of seats for spectators

title—another word for championship

Outfielder Barry Bonds

Index

Published by Creative Education and Creative Paperbacks
P.O. Box 227, Mankato, Minnesota 56002
Creative Education and Creative Paperbacks are imprints of
The Creative Company
www.thecreativecompany.us

Art Direction by Tom Morgan
Book production by Ciara Beitlich
Edited by Jill Kalz

Photographs by AP Images (Tony Tomsic), Corbis (Mark Cunningham, Focus on Sport, Rich Pilling), Dreamstime (Rudi1976), Getty (Bettmann, Thearon W. Henderson, Andy Lyons, MLB Photos, National Baseball Hall of Fame, Rich Pilling, Joe Sargent), Library of Congress (PIC)

Library of Congress Cataloging-in-Publication Data
Names: Tischler, Joe, author.
Title: Pittsburgh Pirates / Joe Tischler.
Description: Mankato, MN : Creative Education and Creative Paperbacks, [2024] | Series: Creative sports. World Series champions | Includes index. | Audience: Ages 7-10 | Audience: Grades 2-3 | Summary: "Elementary-level text and engaging sports photos highlight the Pittsburgh Pirates' MLB World Series wins and losses, plus sensational players associated with the professional baseball team such as Andrew McCutchen."-- Provided by publisher.
Identifiers: LCCN 2023011797 (print) | LCCN 2023011798 (ebook) | ISBN 9781640268333 (library binding) | ISBN 9781682773833 (paperback) | ISBN 9781640269866 (pdf)
Subjects: LCSH: Pittsburgh Pirates (Baseball team)--History--Juvenile literature. | World Series (Baseball)--History--Juvenile literature.
Classification: LCC GV875.P5 T57 2024 (print) | LCC GV875.P5 (ebook) | DDC 796.357/640974886--dc23/eng/20230314
LC record available at https://lccn.loc.gov/2023011797
LC ebook record available at https://lccn.loc.gov/2023011798

Printed in China

WORLD SERIES CHAMPIONS

PITTSBURGH PIRATES

JOE TISCHLER

CREATIVE SPORTS

CREATIVE EDUCATION / CREATIVE PAPERBACKS

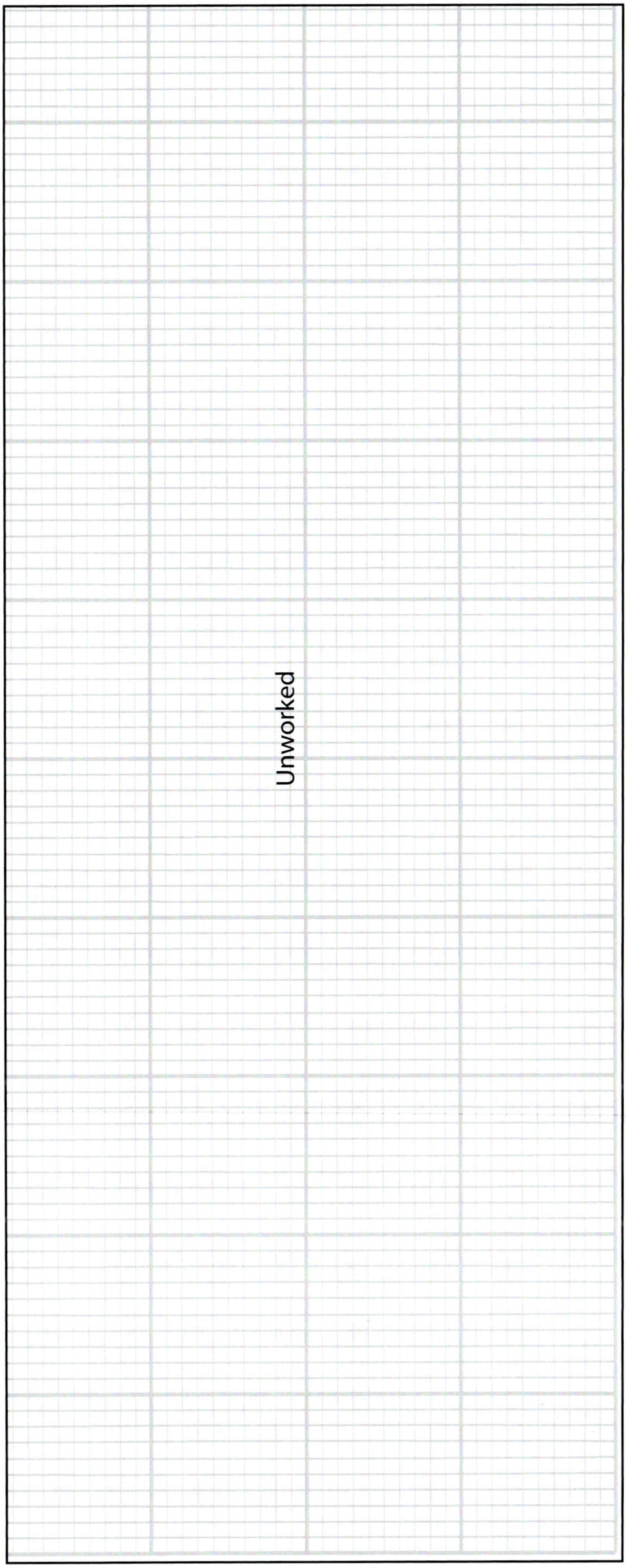

← **Base Support**
(40 x 98 threads)

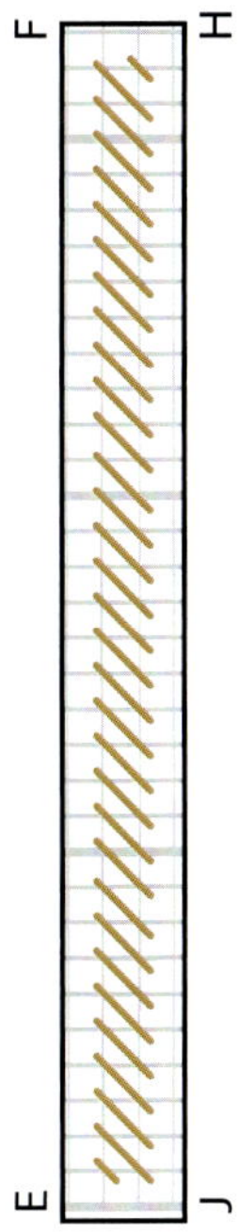

Bottom of Beam Piece (cut 2)
(4 x 34 threads)

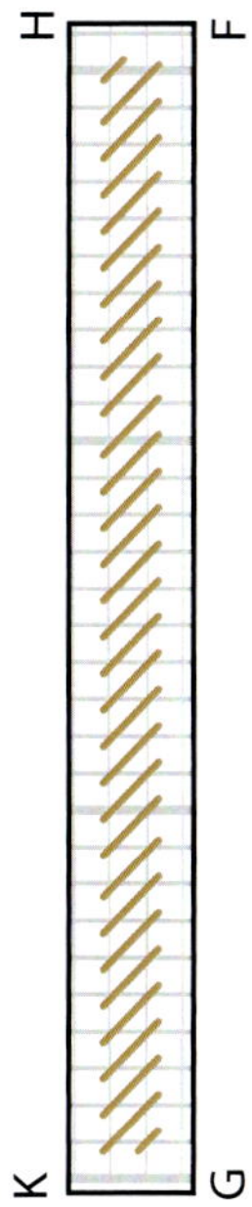

Back of Post Piece (cut 2)
(4 x 32 threads)

Left Peak Ceiling
(26 x 18 threads)

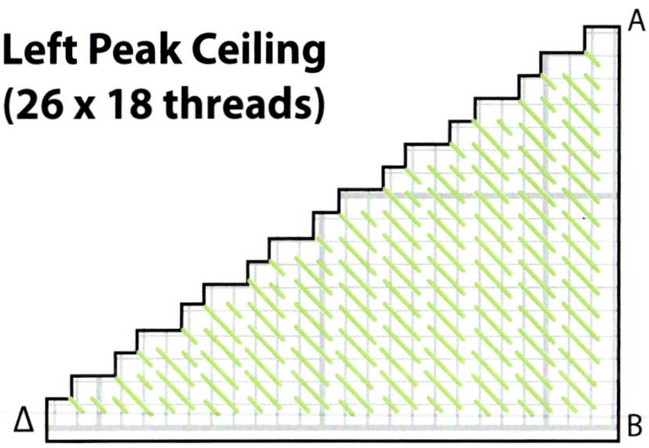

Right Peak Ceiling
(26 x 18 threads)

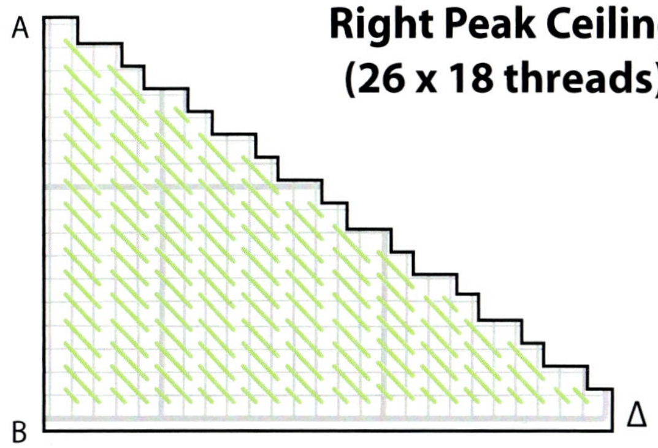

Interior Right
(41 x 79 threads)

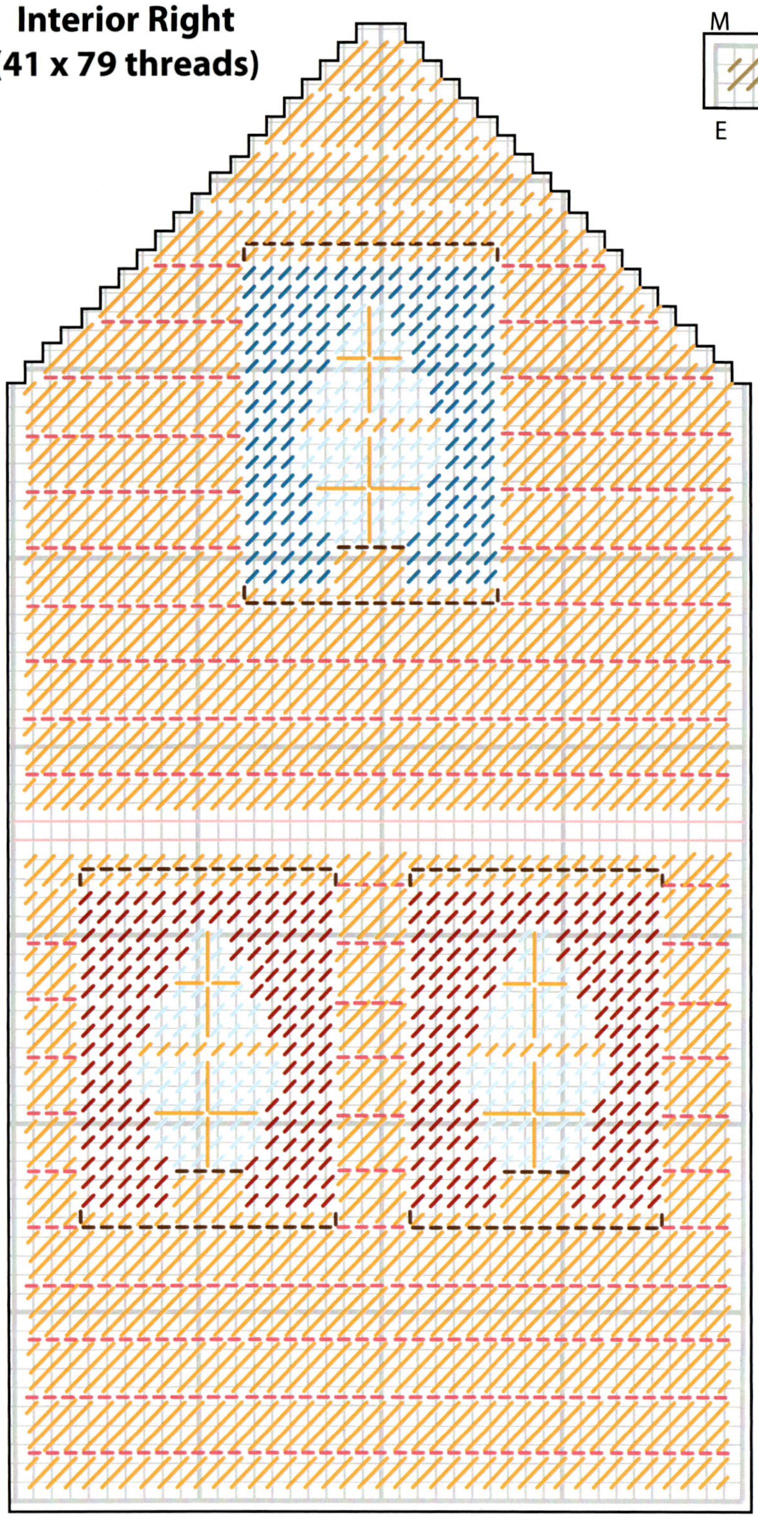

Post/Beam
Left Side Piece
(cut 2)
(37 x 35 threads)

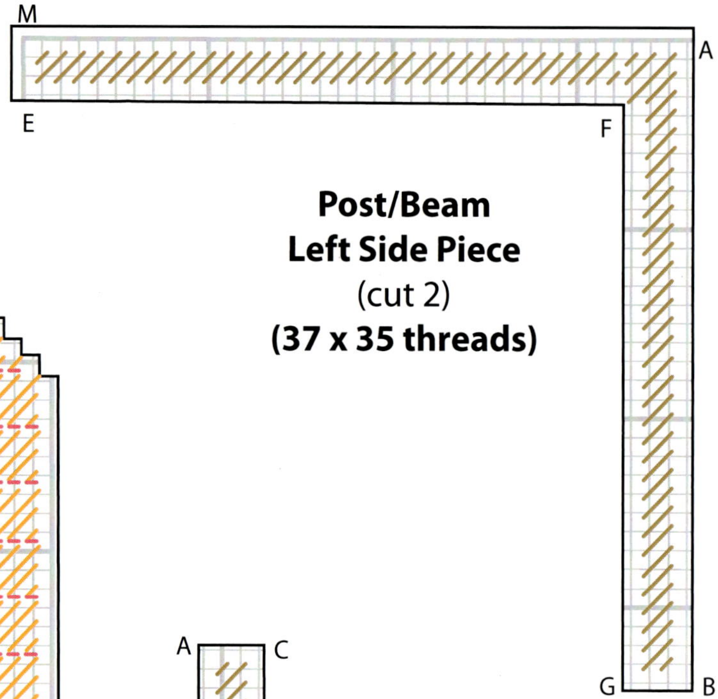

Front of Post
(cut 2)
(4 x 35 threads)

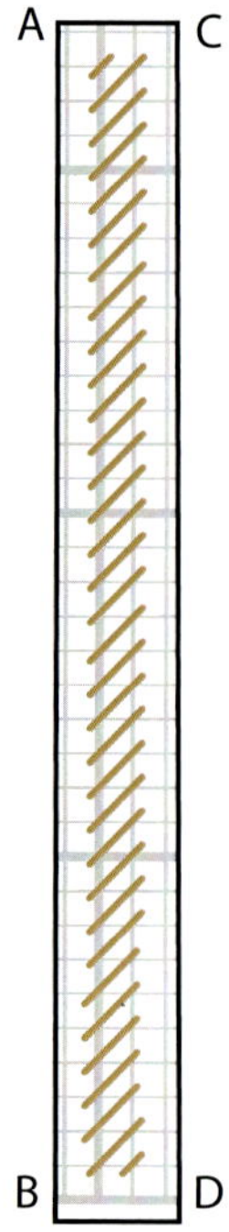

Peak Trim (cut 2)
(26 x 9 threads)

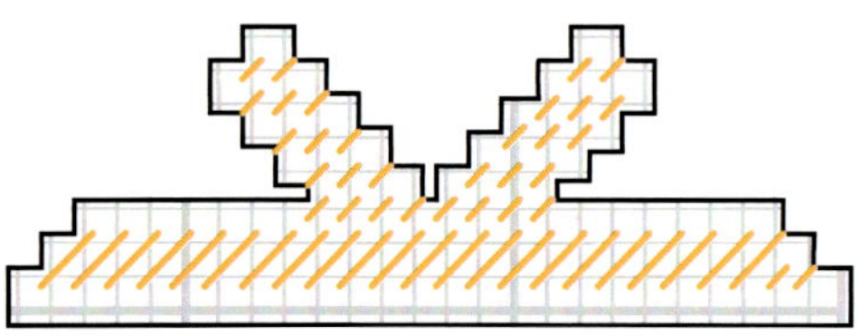

Post/Beam
Right Side Piece
(cut 2)
(37 x 35 threads)

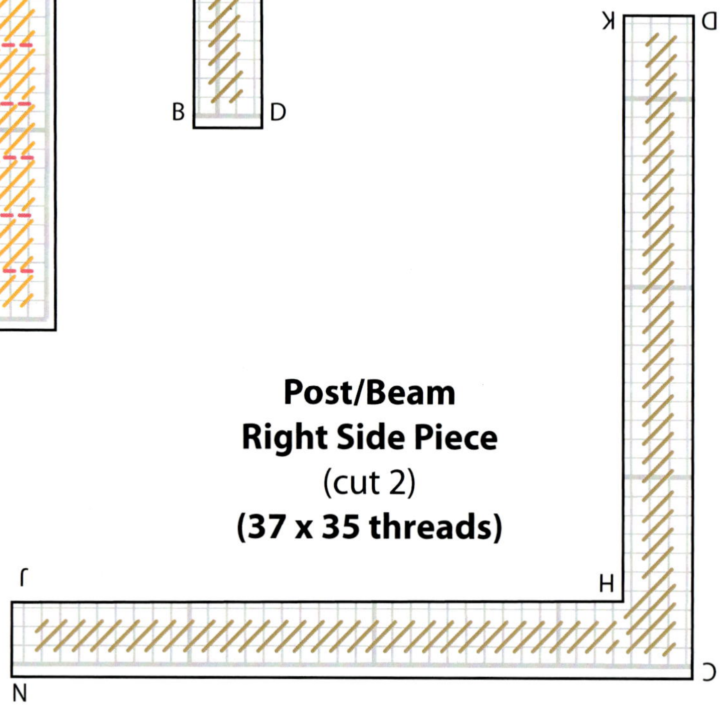

Interior Front
(80 x 98 threads)

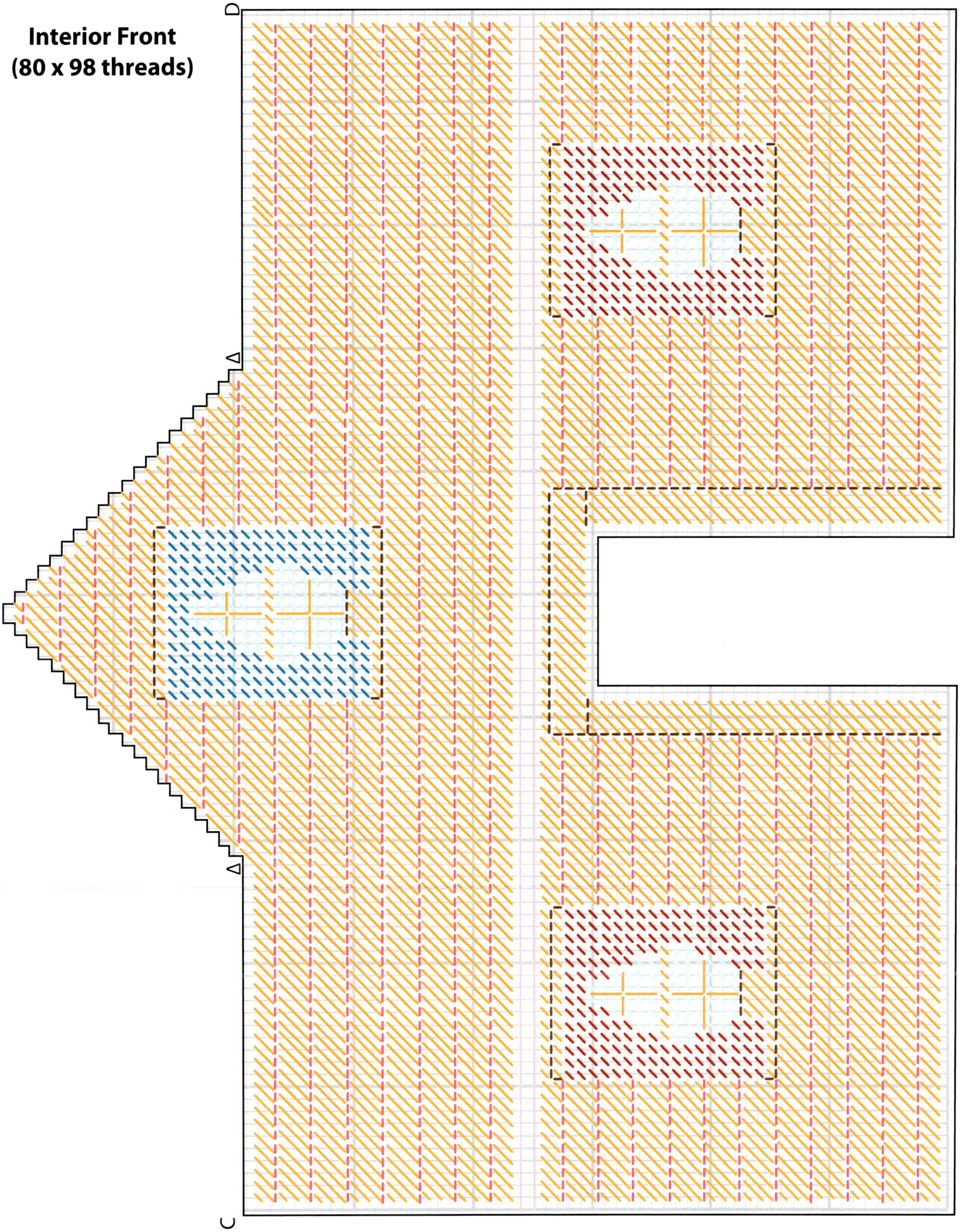

Mantel Left Side
(4 x 8 threads)

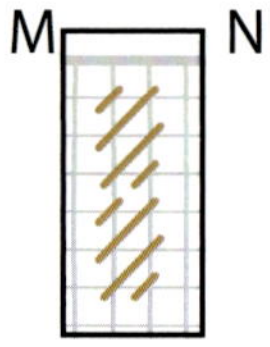

Fireplace Left
(6 x 19 threads)

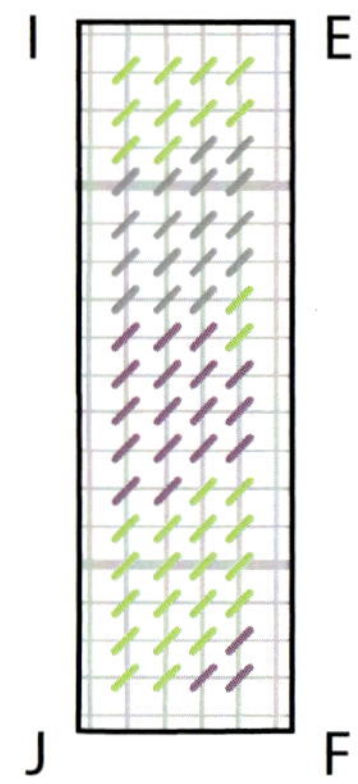

Front Fire
(11 x 8 threads)

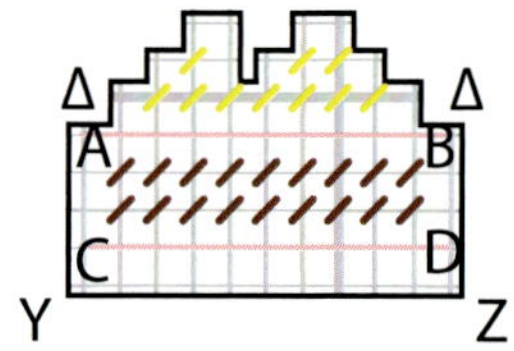

Mantel Top
(26 x 8 threads)

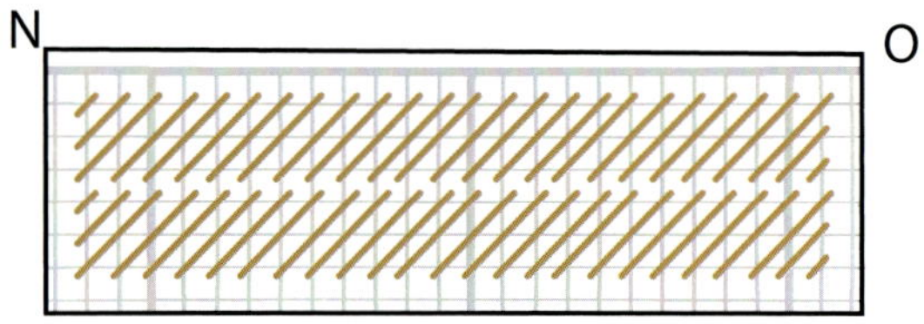

Fireplace Front
(21 x 19 threads)

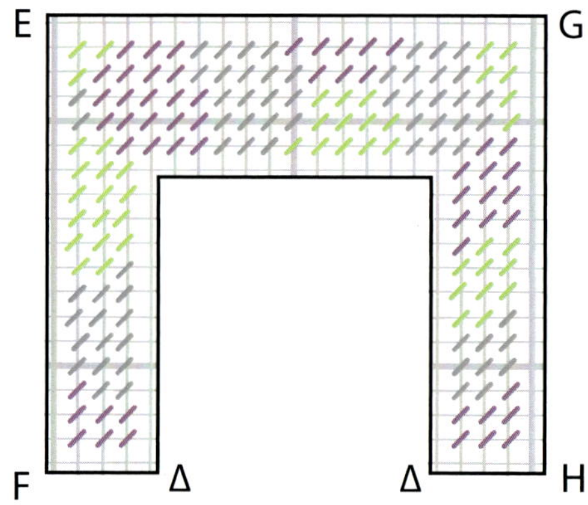

Fireplace Right
(6 x 19 threads)

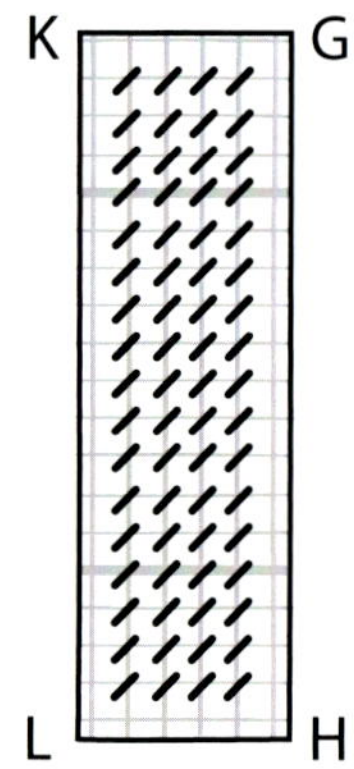

Mantel Right Side
(4 x 8 threads)

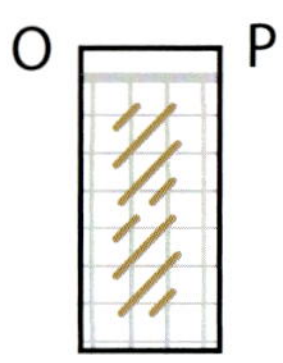

Mantel Front
(26 x 4 threads)

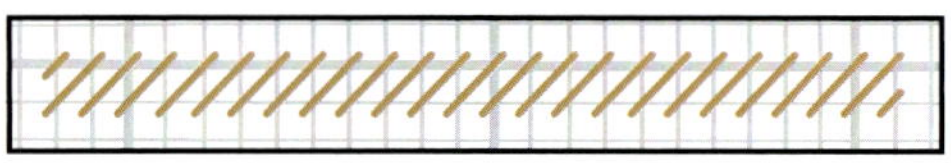

Inner Chimney
Cap Edge (cut 4)
(8 x 3 threads)

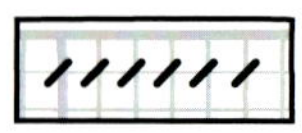

Outer Chimney
Cap Edge (cut 4)
(12 x 4 threads)

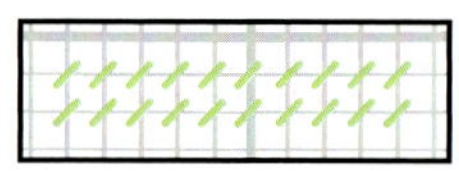

Mantel Bottom
(26 x 8 threads)

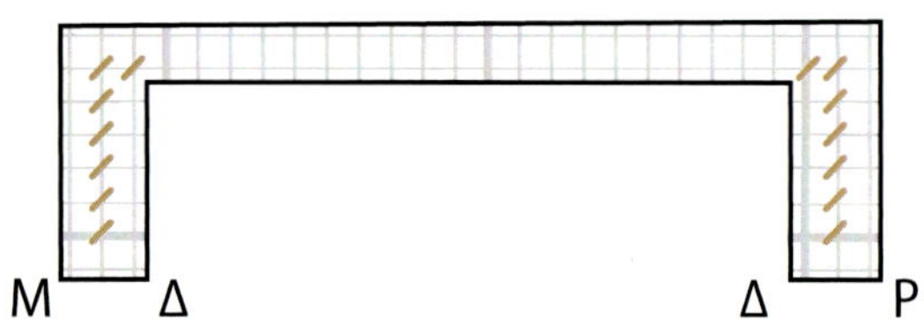

Chimney Cap Bottom
(8 x 8 threads)

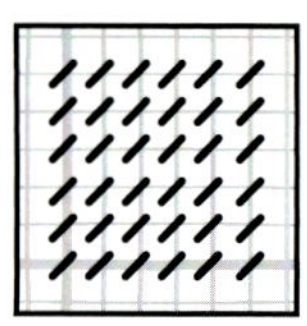

Chimney Cap Top
(12 x 12 threads)

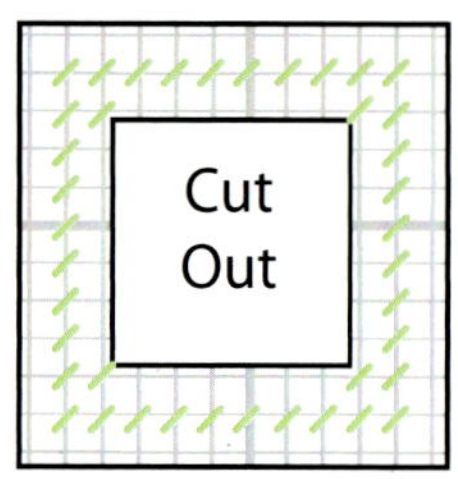

Interior Left
(41 x 79 threads)

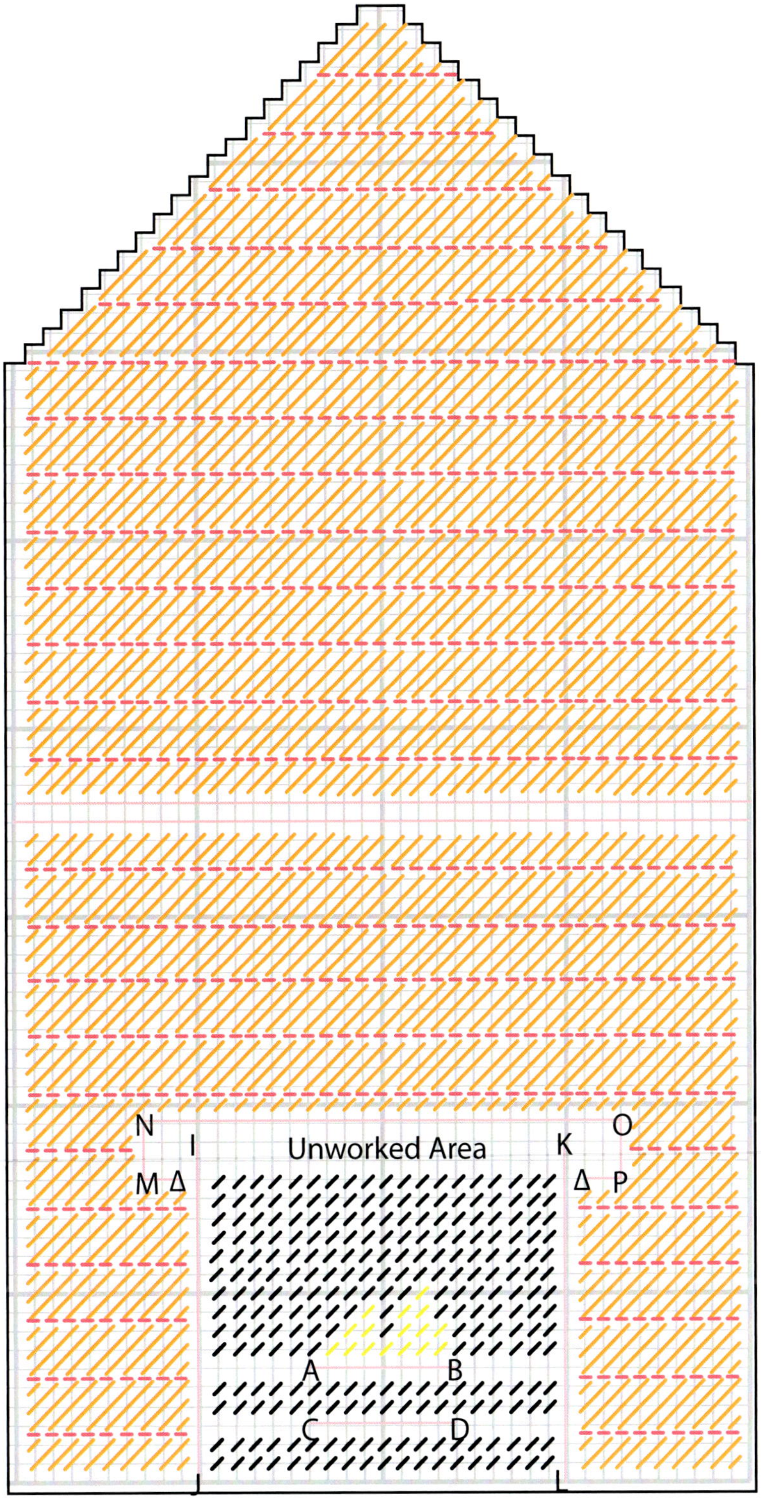

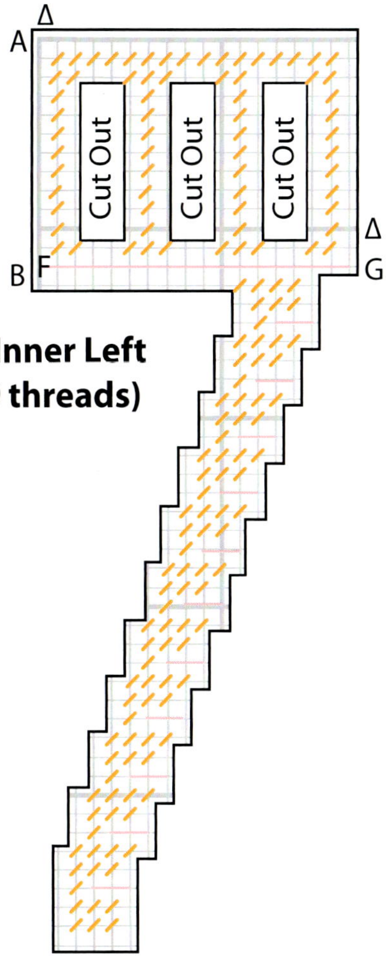

Ladder Inner Left
(18 x 49 threads)

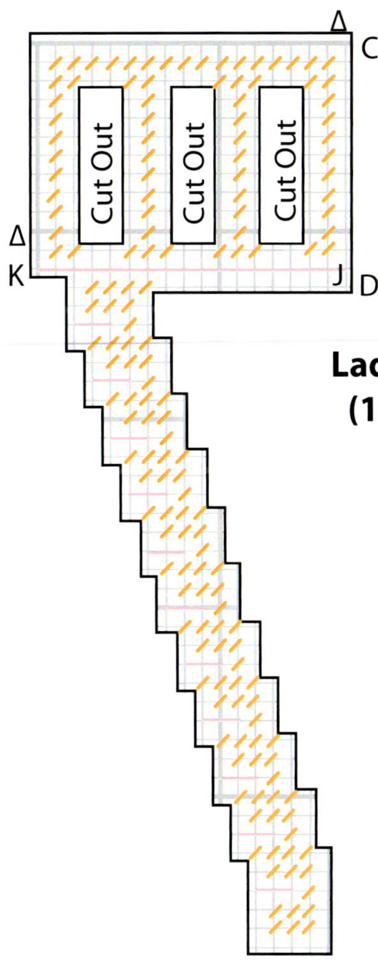

Ladder Inner Right
(18 x 49 threads)

Step (cut 11)
(12 x 3 threads)

Chimney Front (10 x 91 threads)

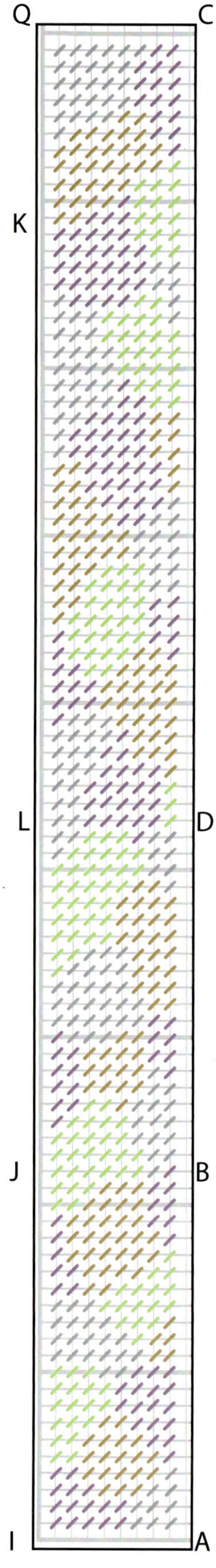

Chimney Back (10 x 91 threads)

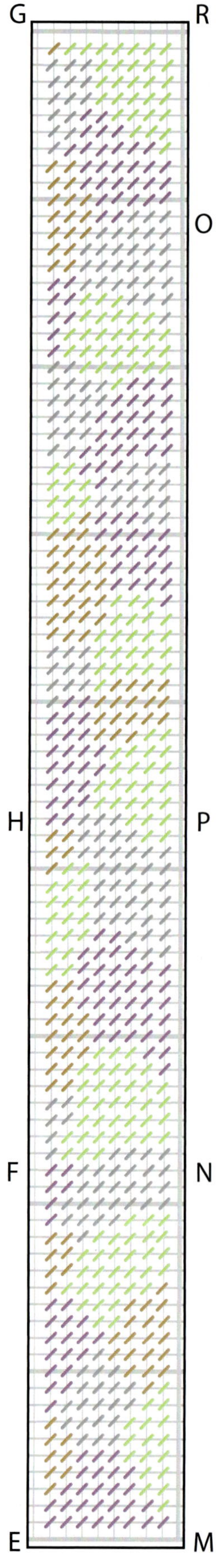

Loft Right (48 x 14 threads)

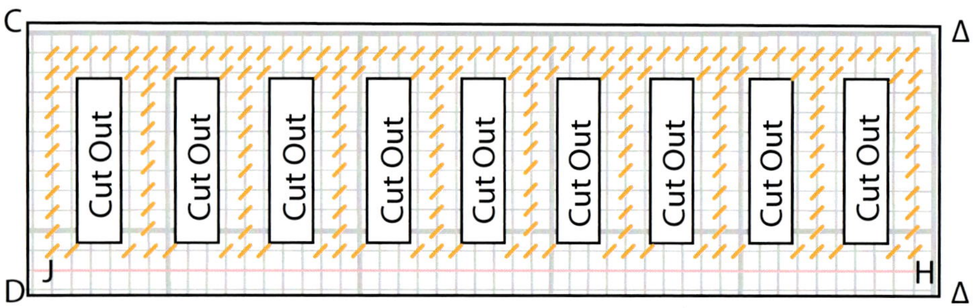

Loft Left (38 x 14 threads)

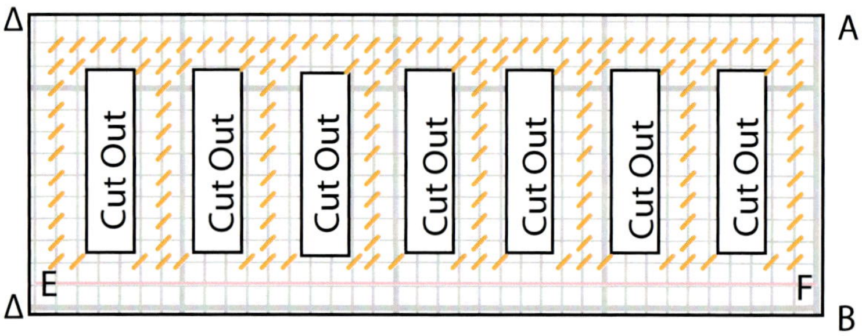

First Floor
(41 x 98 threads)

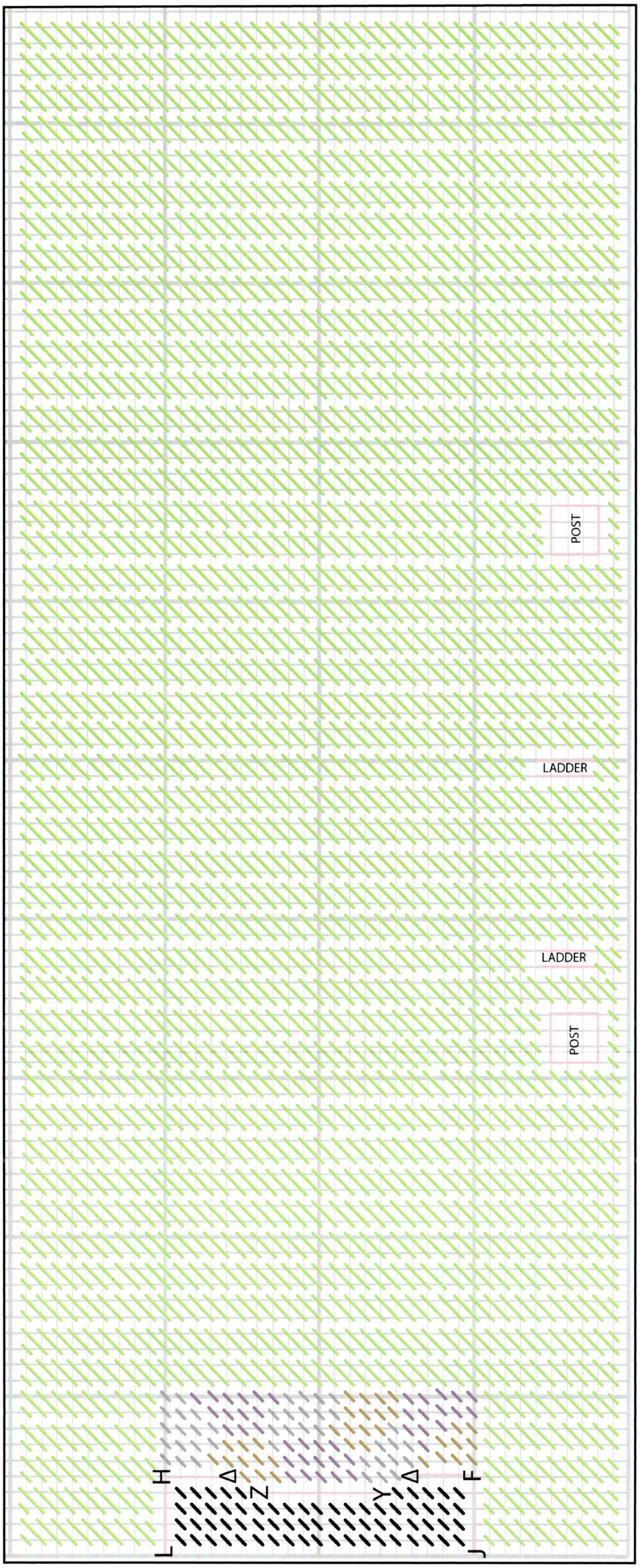

Ladder Outer Left
(15 x 35 threads)

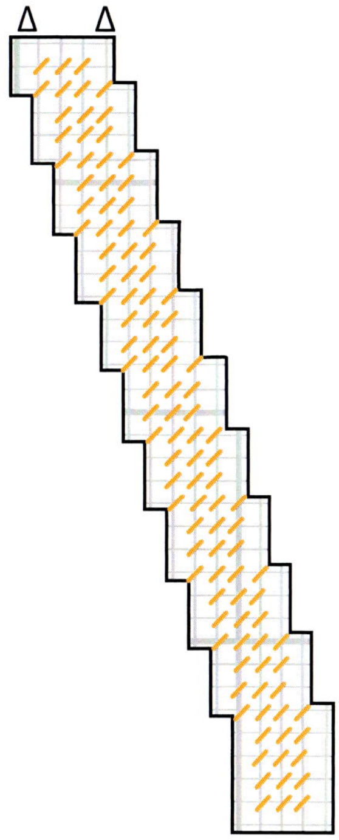

Ladder Outer Right
(15 x 35 threads)

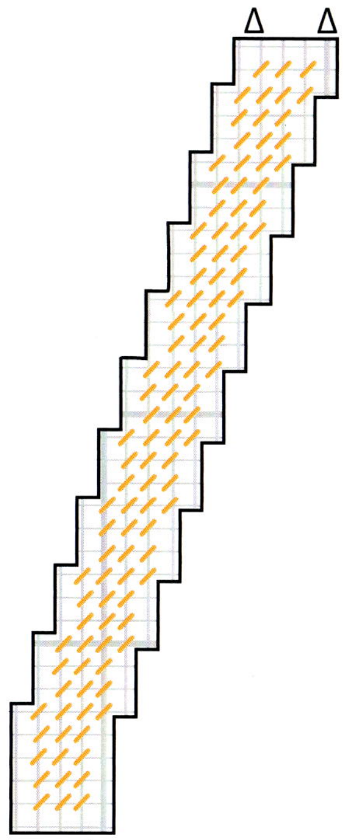

Right Roof
(34 x 23 threads)

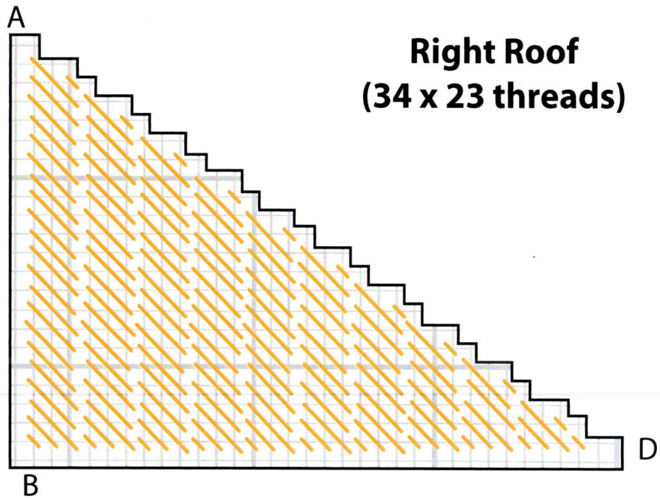

Left Roof
(34 x 23 threads)

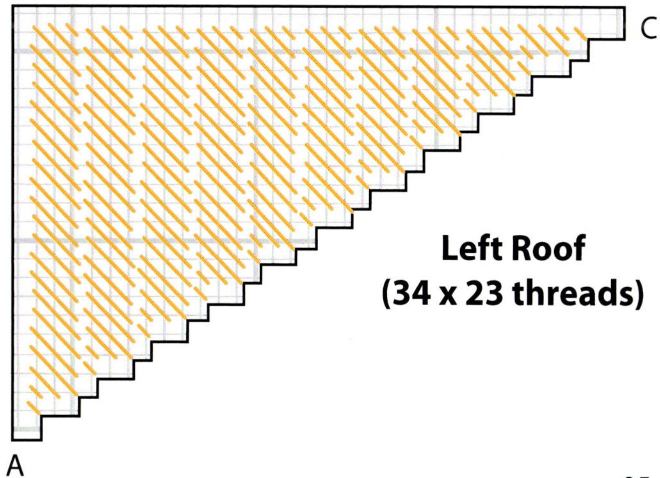

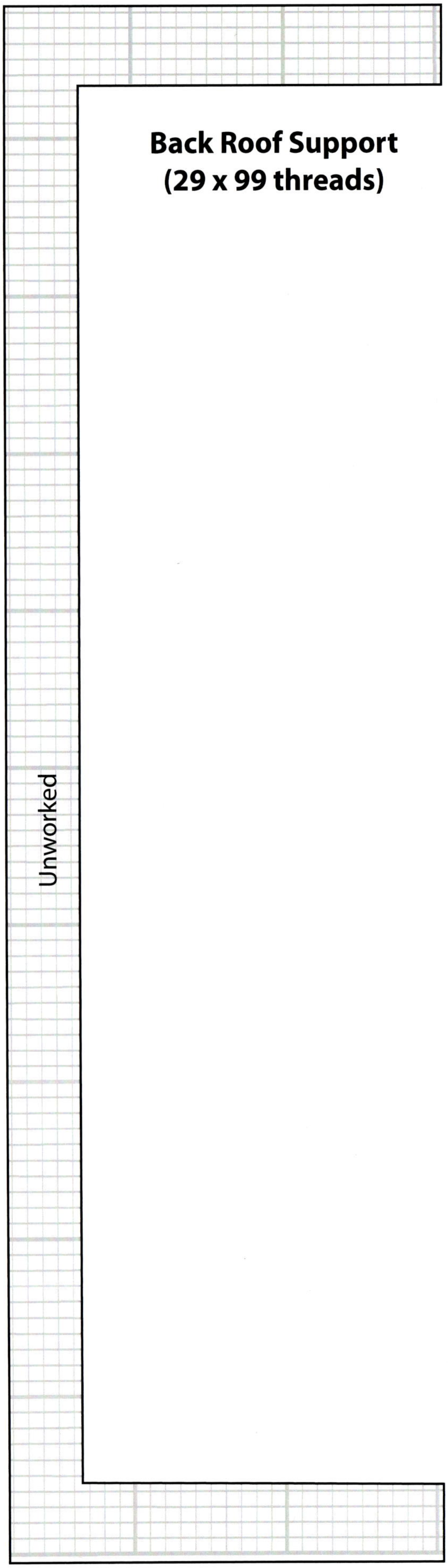

Back Roof Support
(29 x 99 threads)

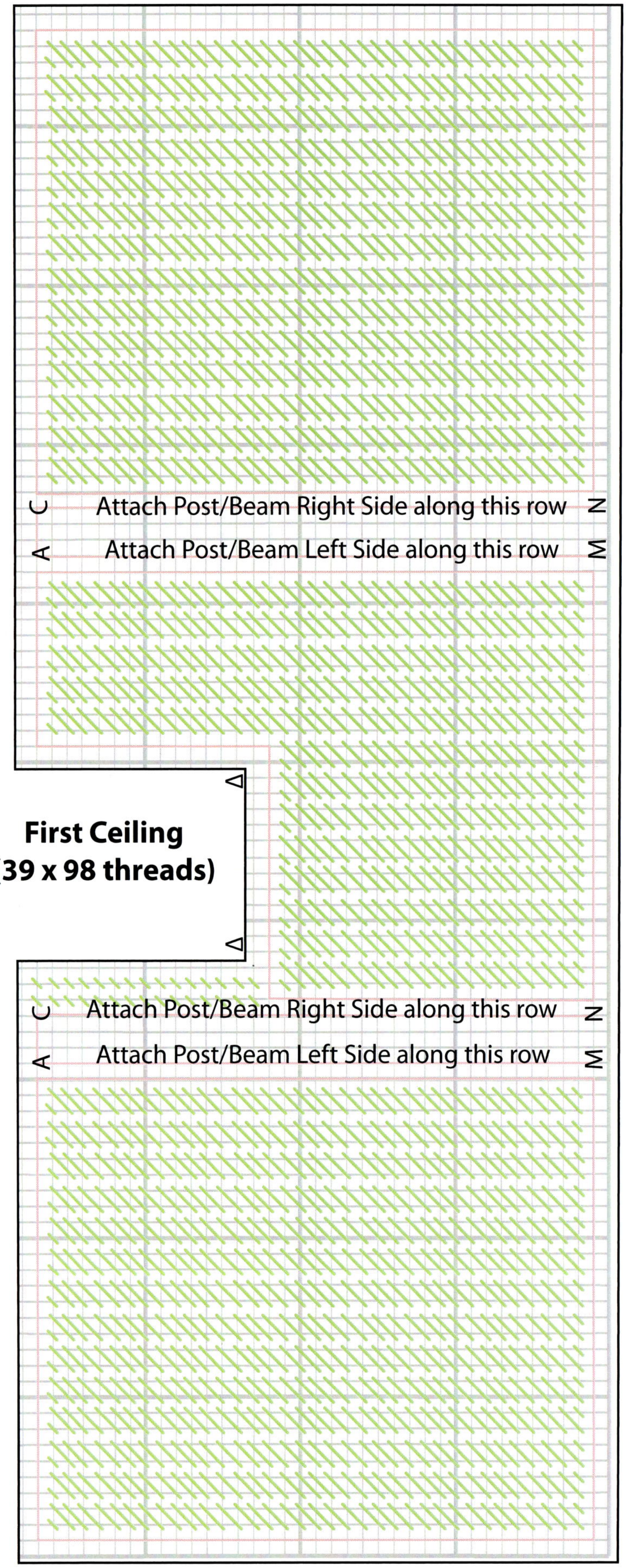

First Ceiling
(39 x 98 threads)

Side Support
(cut 2)
(40 x 77 threads)

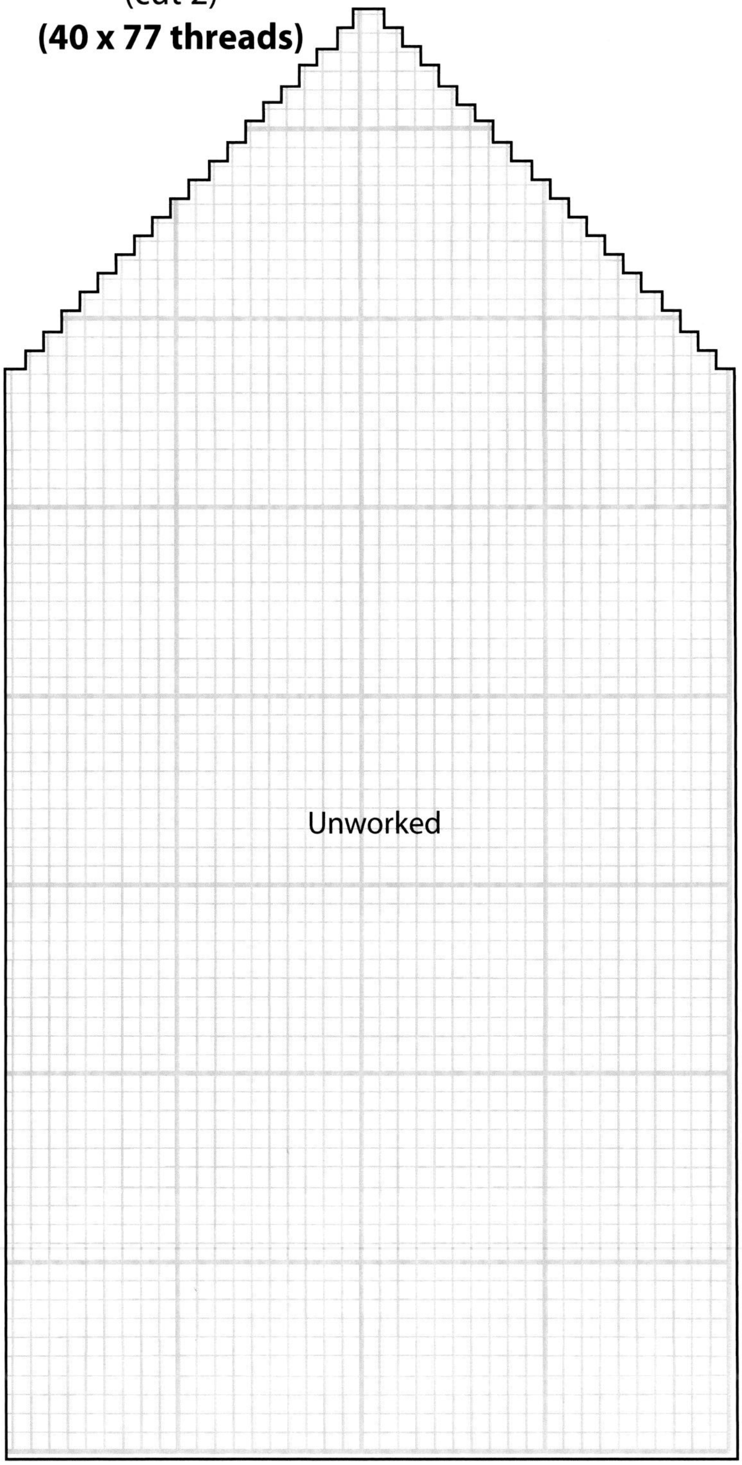

First Ceiling Support (cut 2)
(37 x 30 threads)

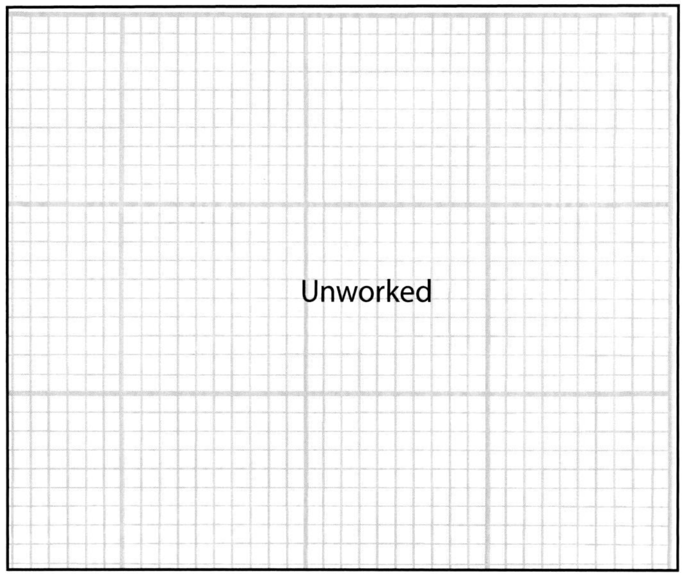

First Ceiling Support
(37 x 28 threads)

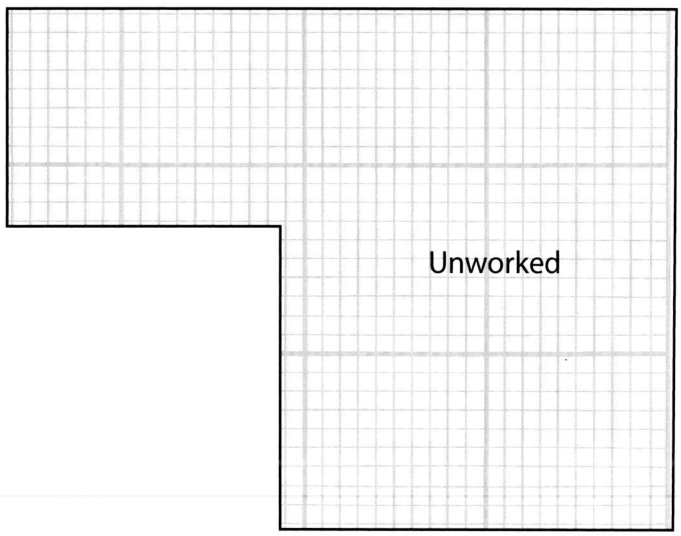

Back Roof (110 x 35 threads)

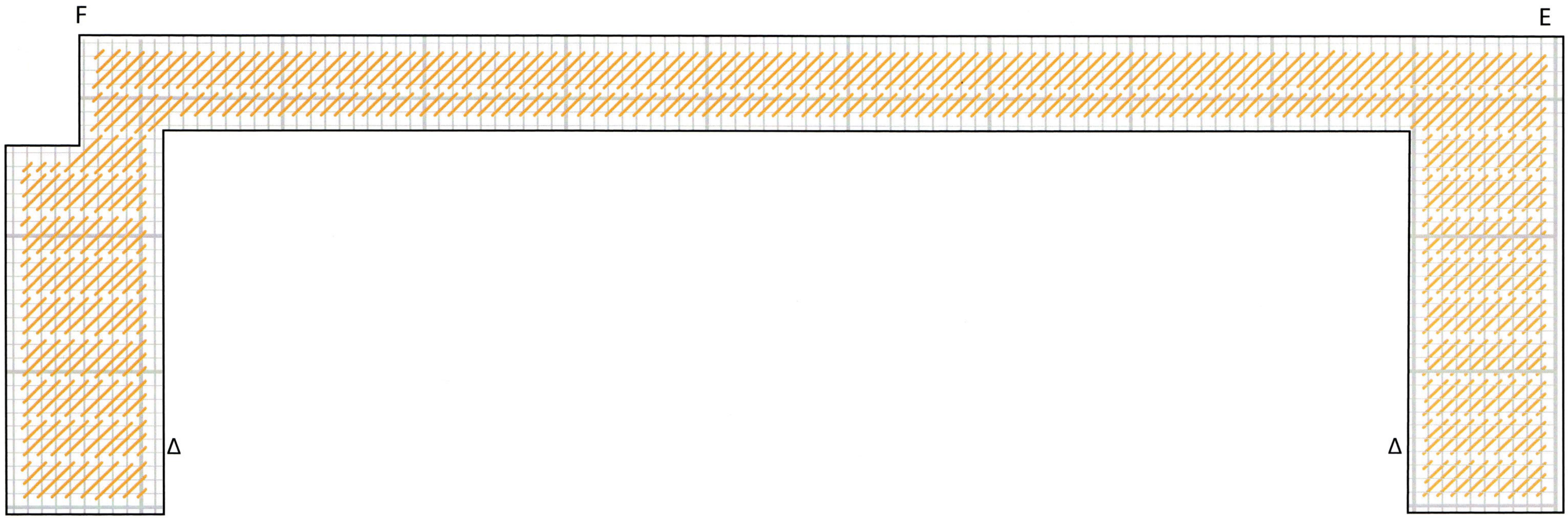

Front Roof (110 x 35 threads)

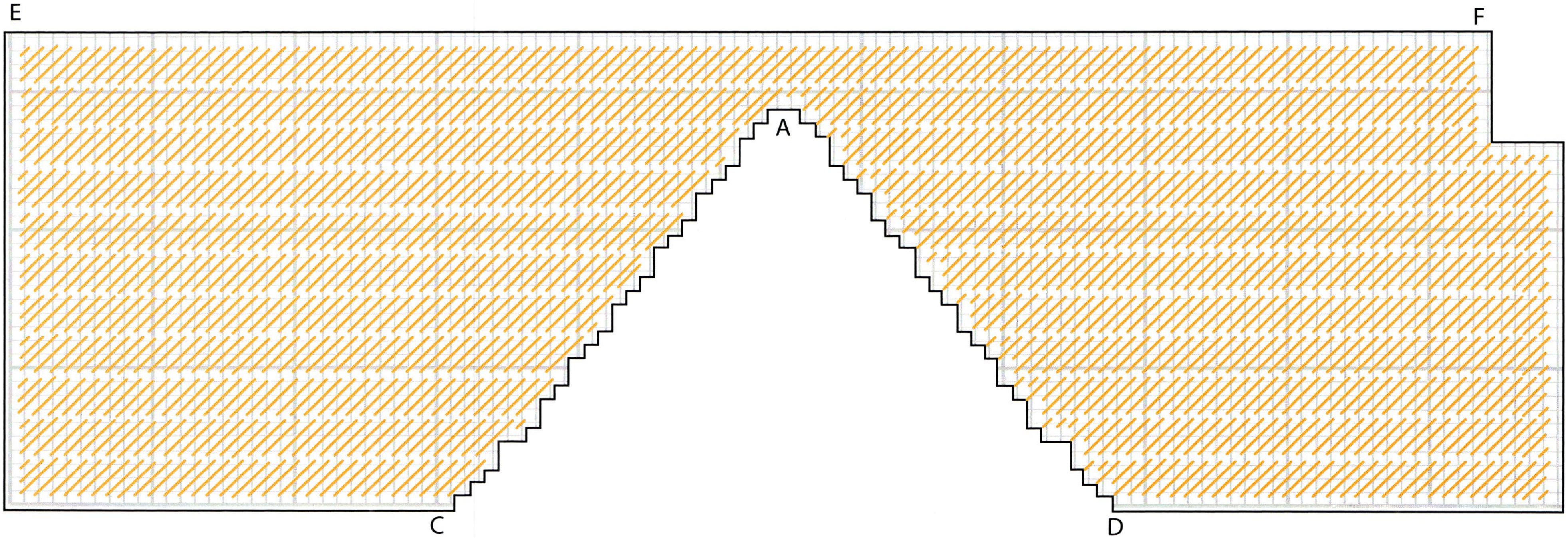

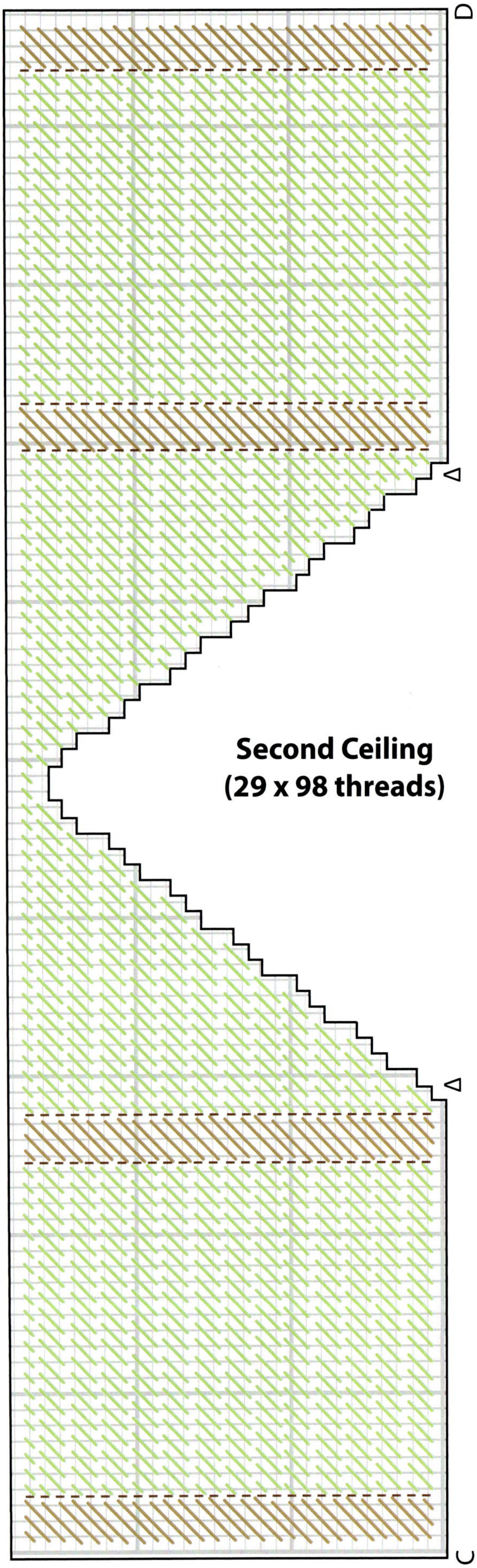

Second Ceiling
(29 x 98 threads)

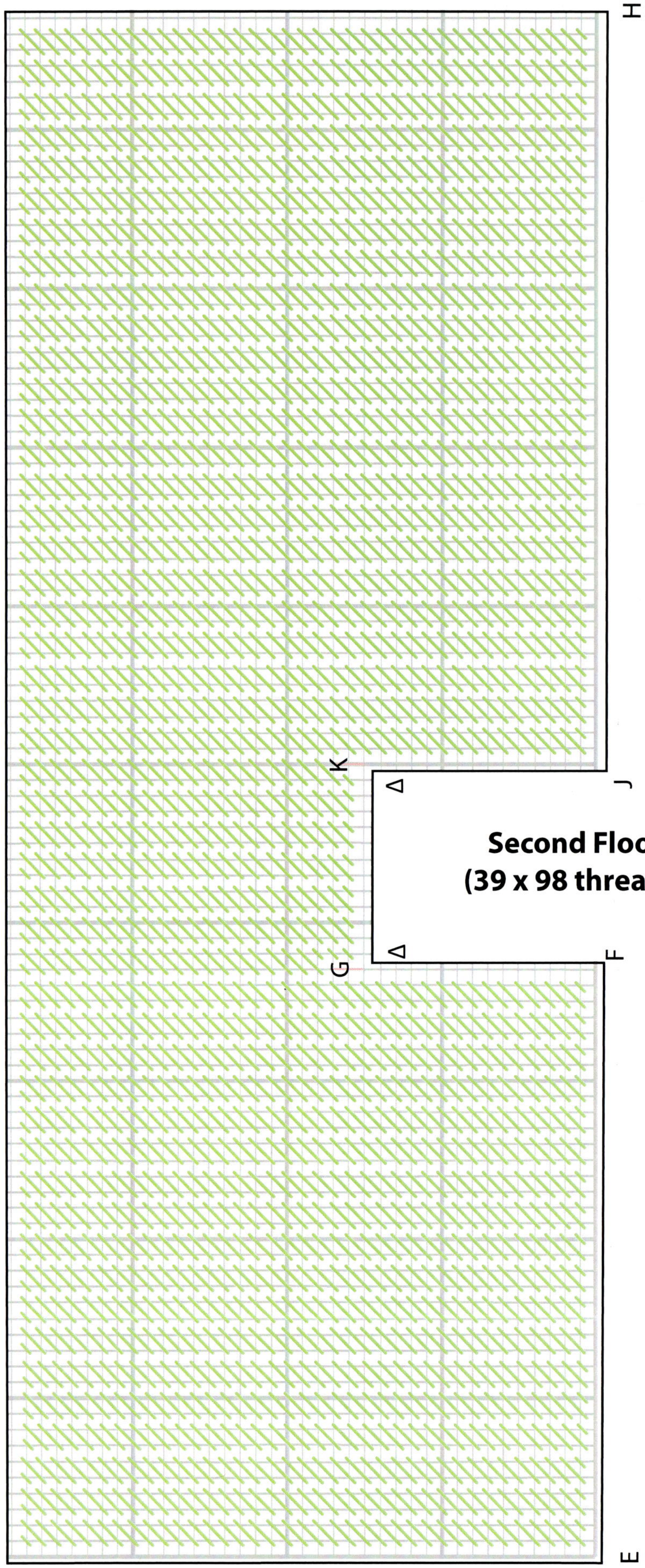

Second Floor
(39 x 98 threads)

Chair Back Leg
(cut 4)
(8 x 16 threads)

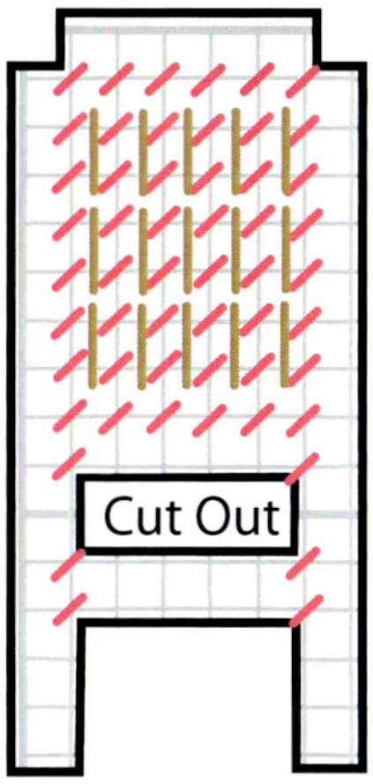

Chair Seat Back
(cut 4)
(8 x 9 threads)

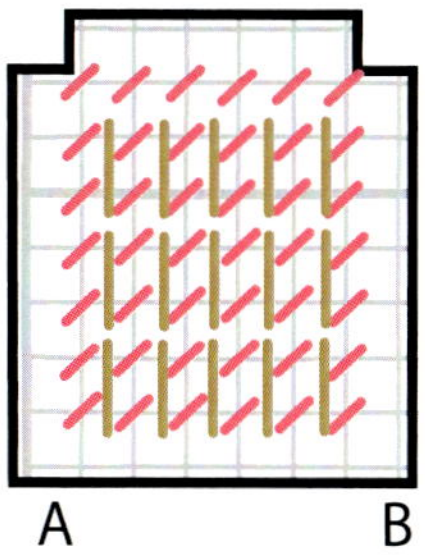

Chair Seat
(cut 4)
(8 x 6 threads)

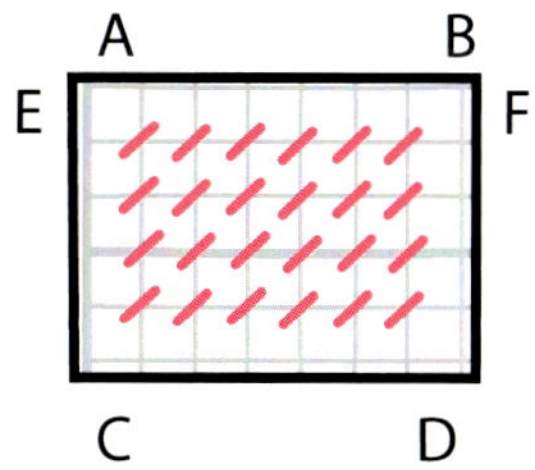

Chair Front Leg
(cut 4)
(8 x 8 threads)

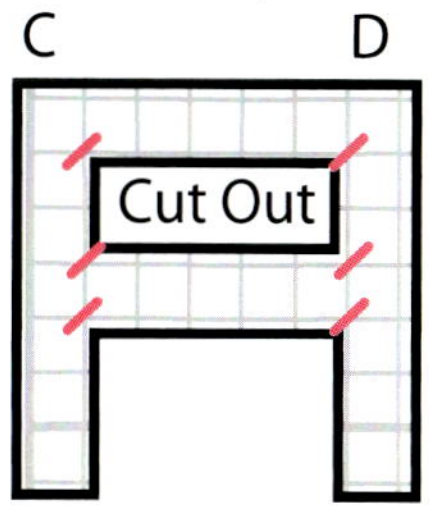

Chair Side Legs
(cut 4 each)
(7 x 8 threads)

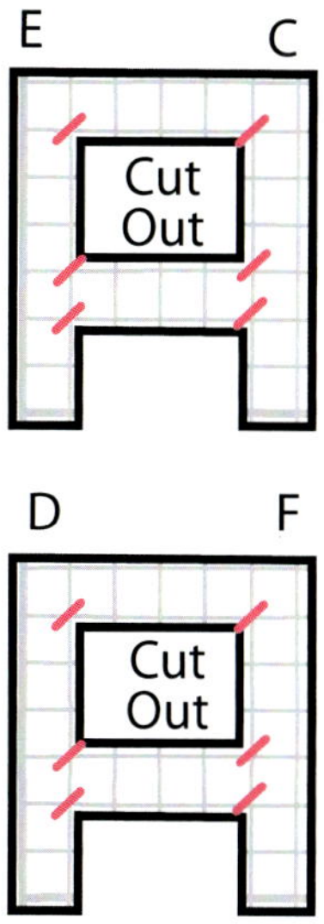

Front Log
(11 x 6 threads)

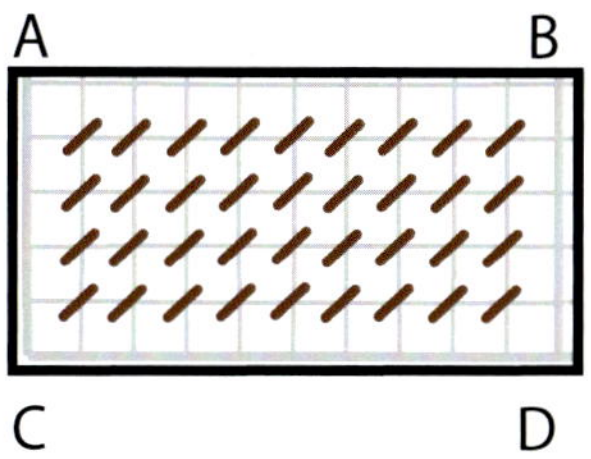

Back Log
(9 x 6 threads)

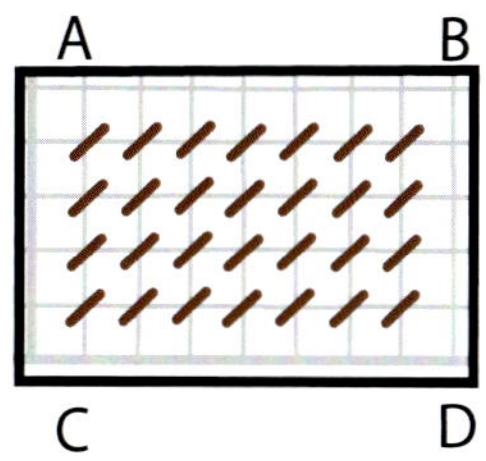

End Table Leg
(cut 2)
(14 x 13 threads)

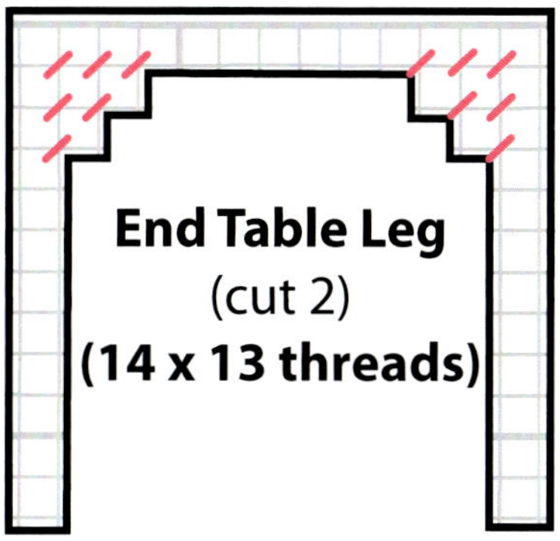

Side Table Leg
(cut 2)
(20 x 13 threads)

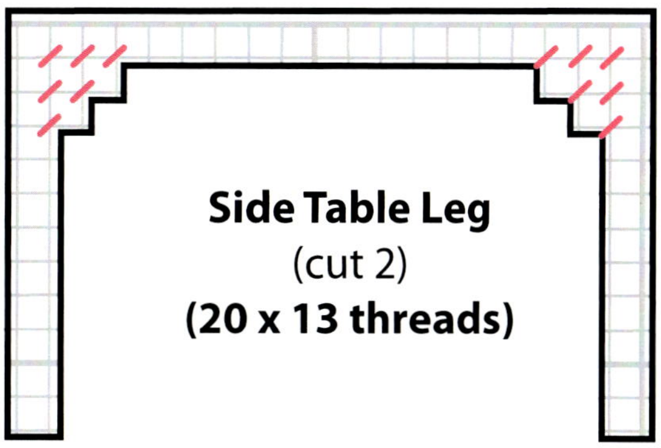

Table Top
(22 x 16 threads)

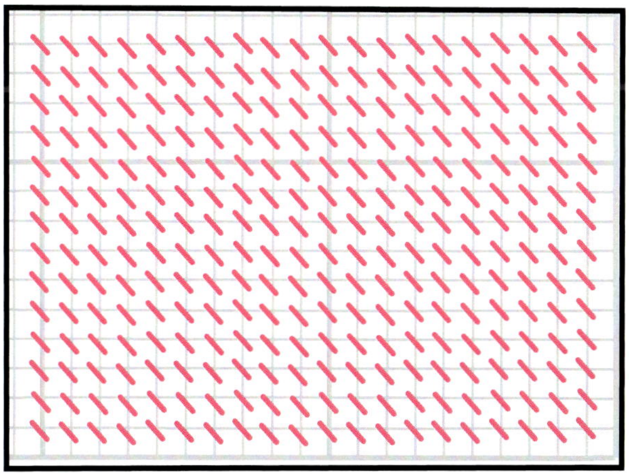

Table Underside
(22 x 16 threads)

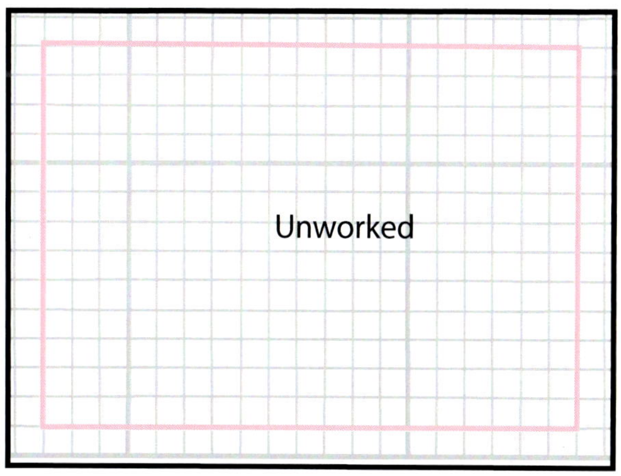

Sink Sides
(8 x 4 threads)

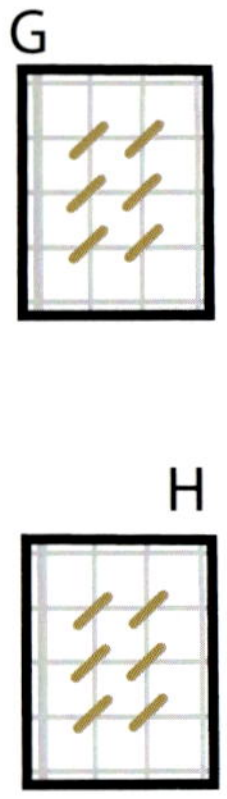

Sink Back
(8 x 4 threads)

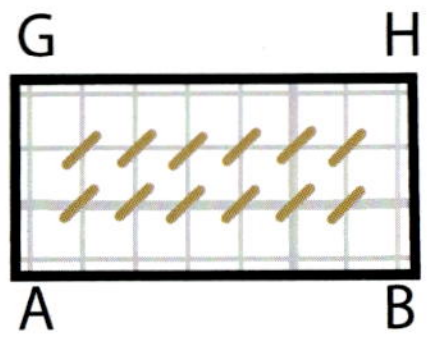

Sink Bottom
(8 x 5 threads)

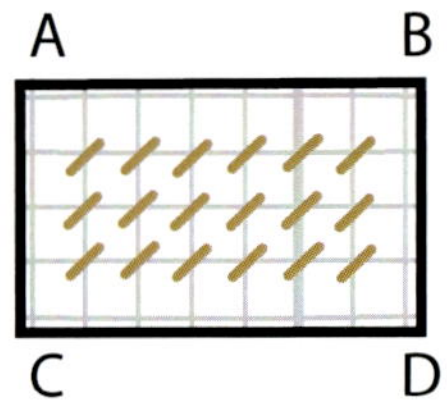

Sink Front
(8 x 4 threads)

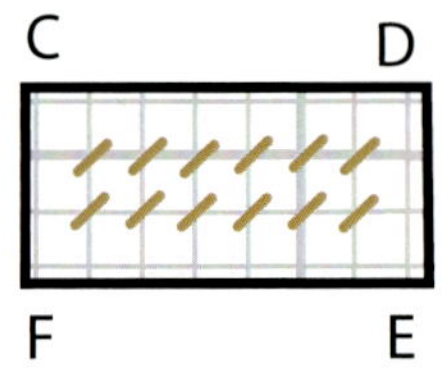

Sink Top
(10 x 7 threads)

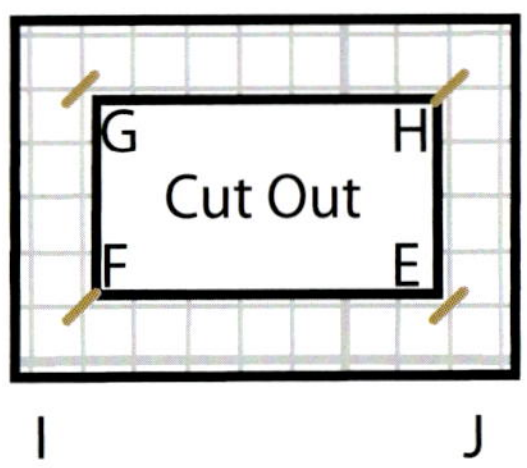

Sink Face
(10 x 5 threads)

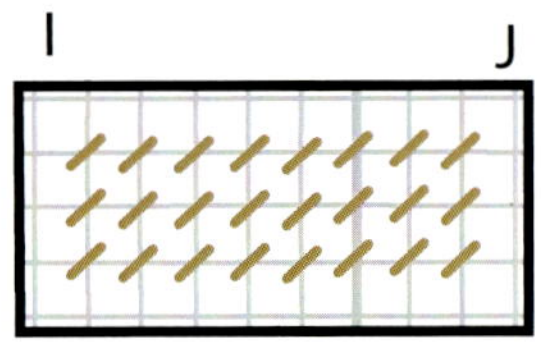

Cabinet Front
(17 x 13 threads)

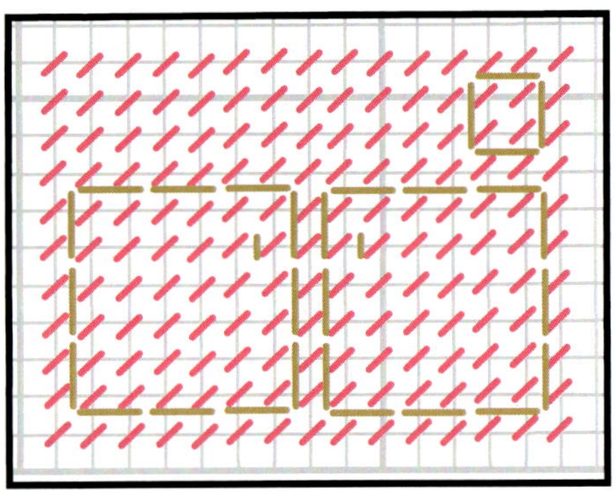

Cabinet Side
(cut 2)
(7 x 13 threads)

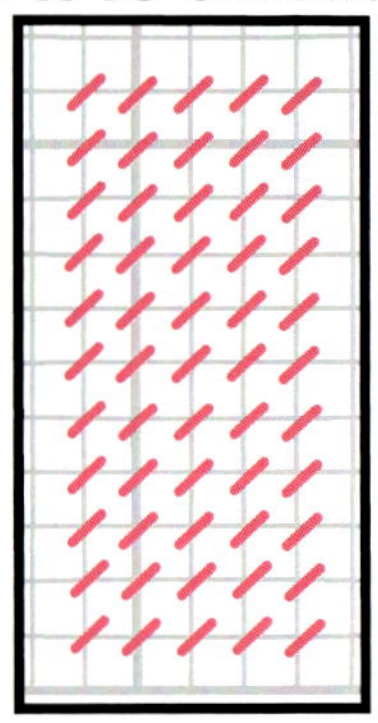

Pump Front
(11 x 11 threads)

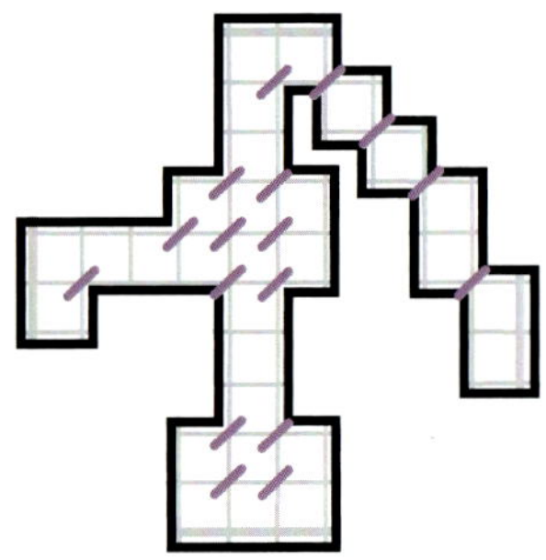

Pump Back
(11 x 11 threads)

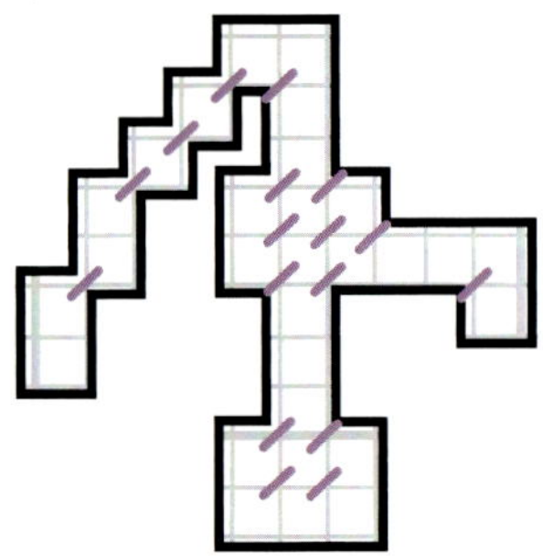

Cabinet Back
(17 x 15 threads)

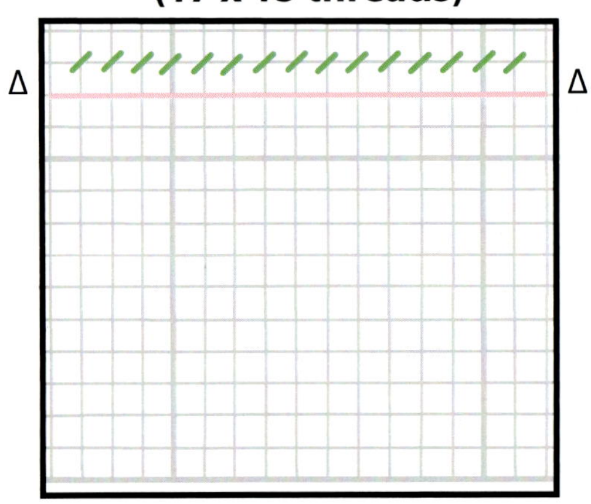

Countertop
(17 x 7 threads)

Stove Fire
(10 x 6 threads)

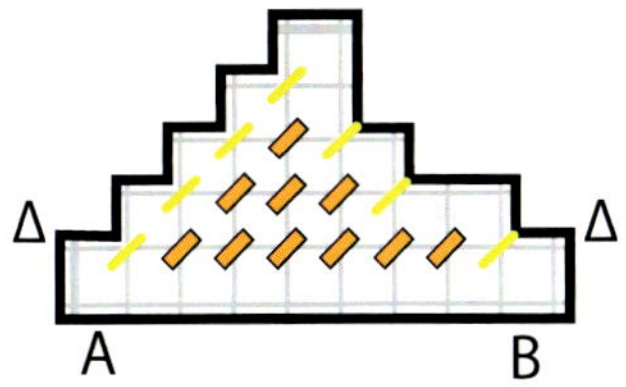

Stove Interior Back
(14 x 10 threads)

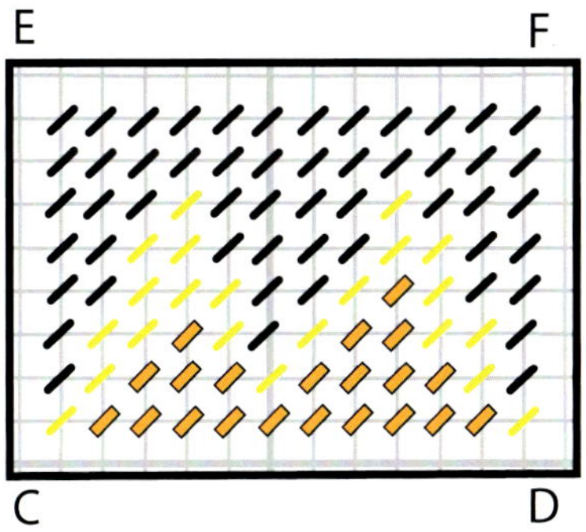

Stove Door
(14 x 9 threads)

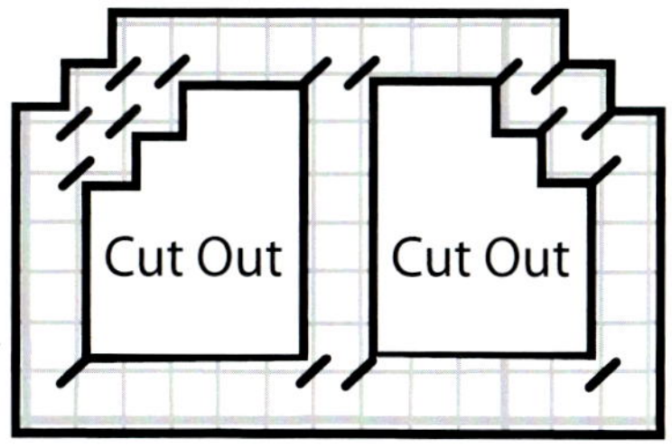

Stove Bottom
(14 x 8 threads)

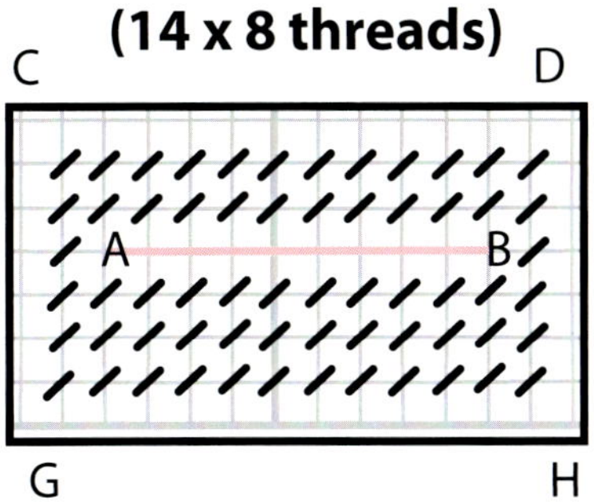

Stove Top
(16 x 9 threads)

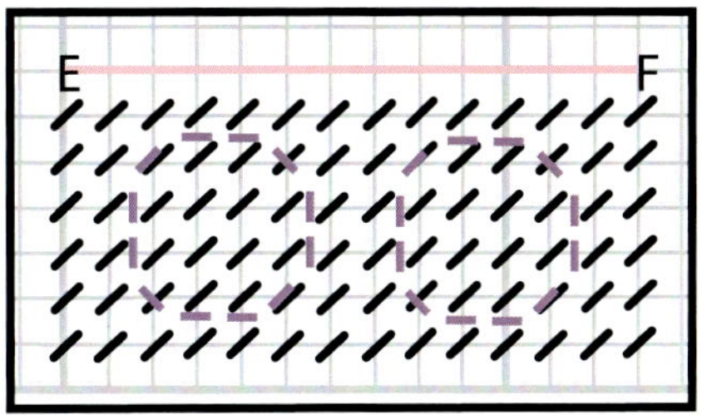

Stove Side
(cut 2)
(9 x 14 threads)

Stove Front
(16 x 14 threads)

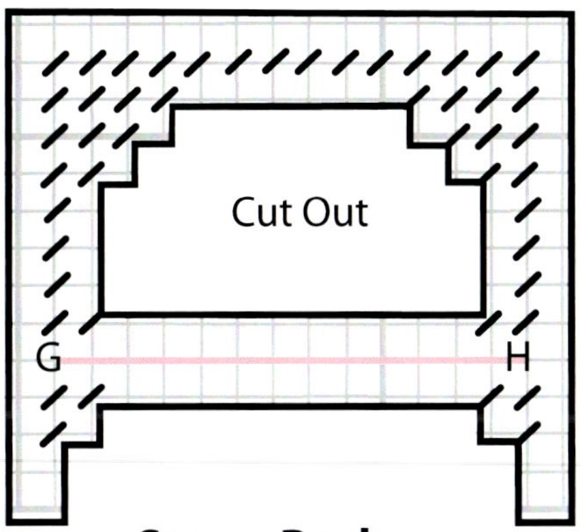

Stove Back
(16 x 14 threads)

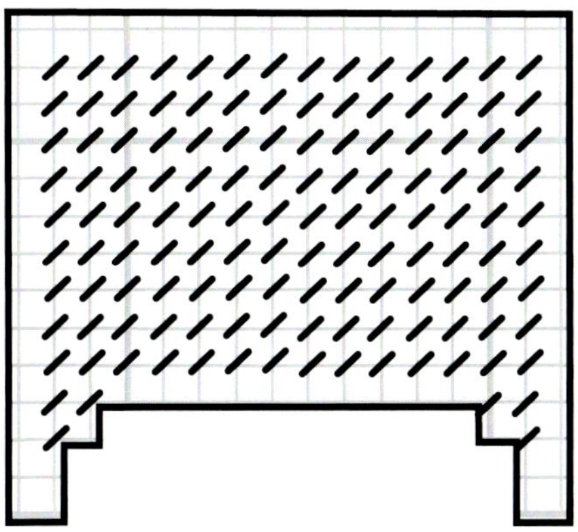

Living Room Rug
(20 x 24 threads)

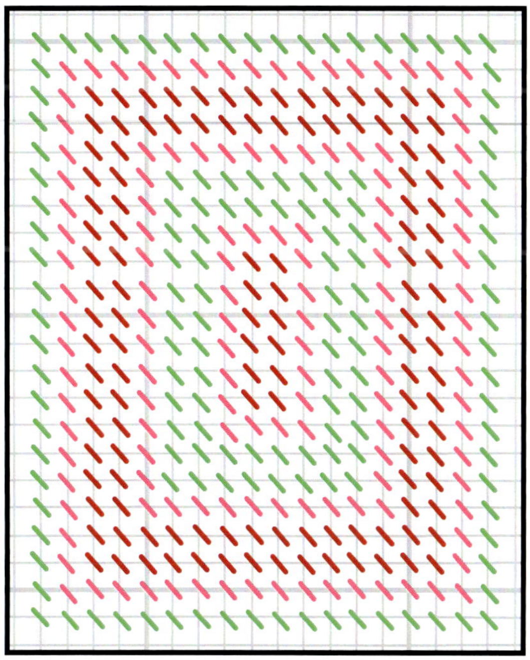

Arm Top
(cut 6)
(7 x 3 threads)

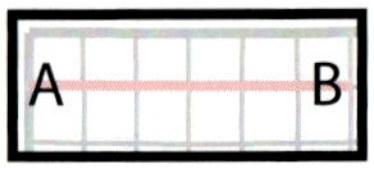

Arm Side
(cut 6)
(7 x 4 threads)

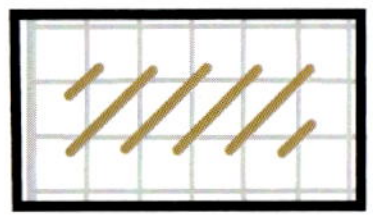

Left Side
(cut 3)
(9 x 15 threads)

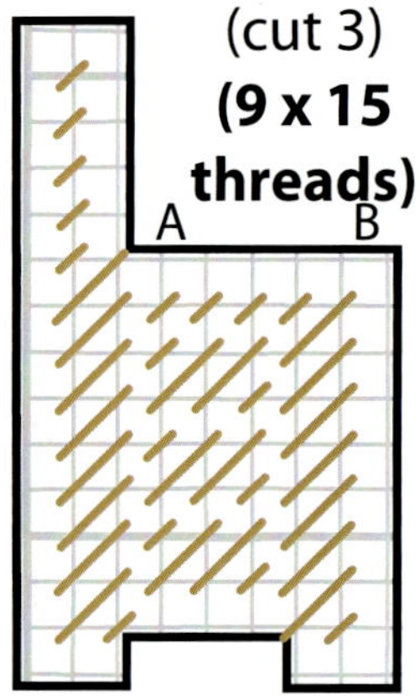

Right Side
(cut 3)
(9 x 15 threads)

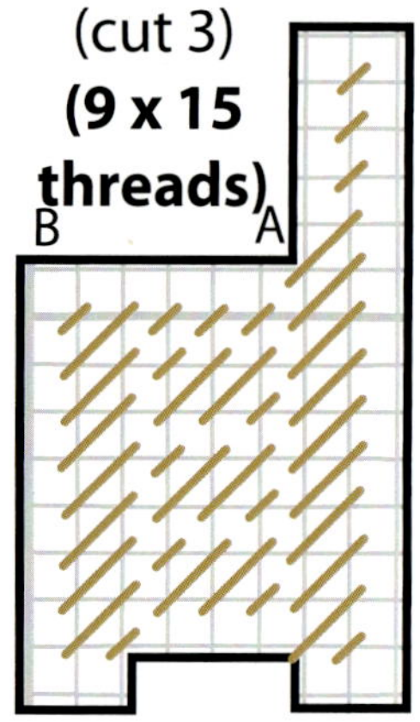

Chair Top (cut 2)
(12 x 3 threads)

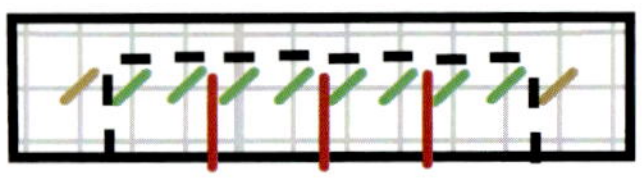

Chair Seat (cut 2)
(10 x 7 threads)

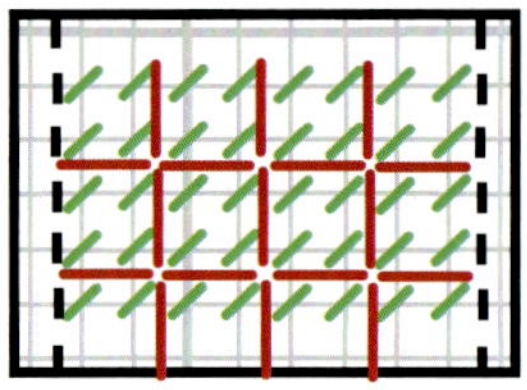

Chair Back Cushion (cut 2)
(12 x 9 threads)

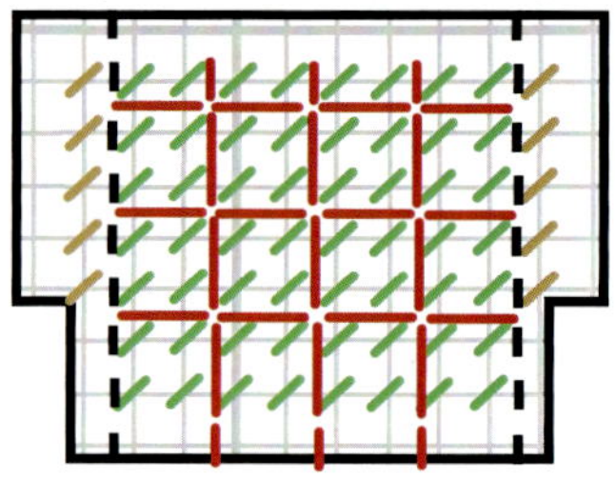

Chair Back
(cut 2)
(12 x 15 threads)

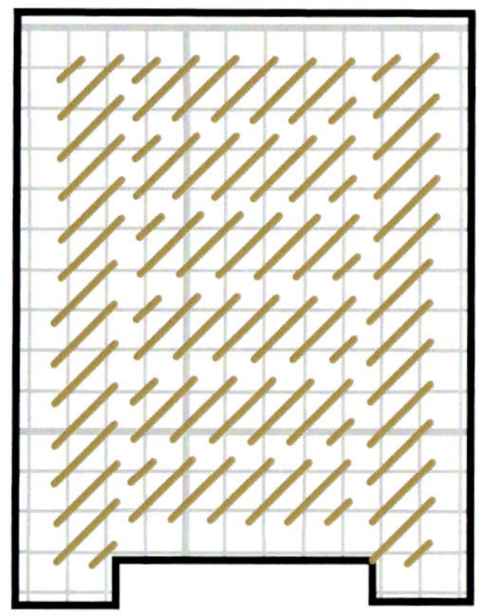

Sofa Back
(25 x 15 threads)

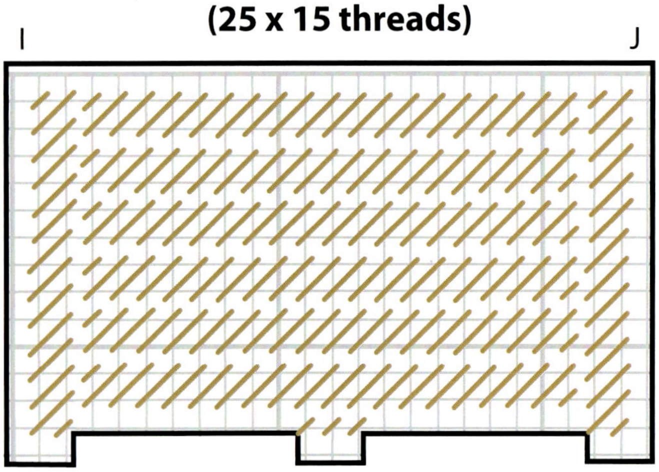

Chair Front (cut 2)
(12 x 10 threads)

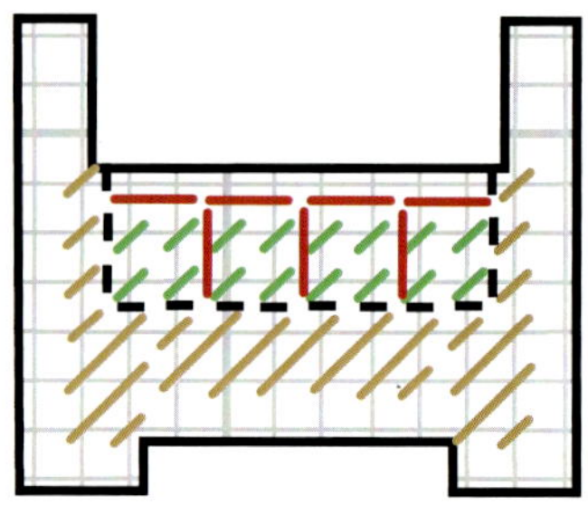

Sofa Top
(25 x 3 threads)

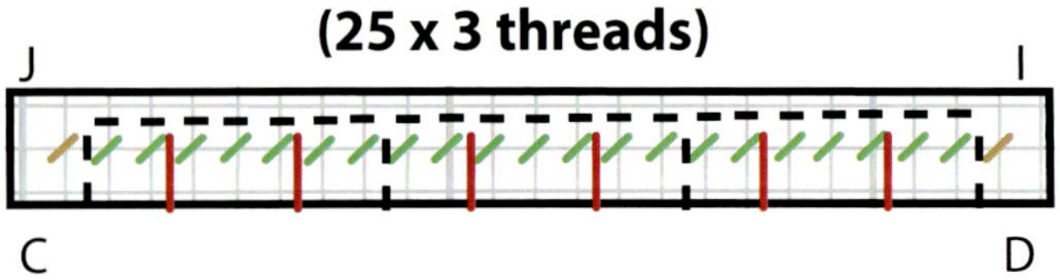

Sofa Back Cushion
(25 x 9 threads)

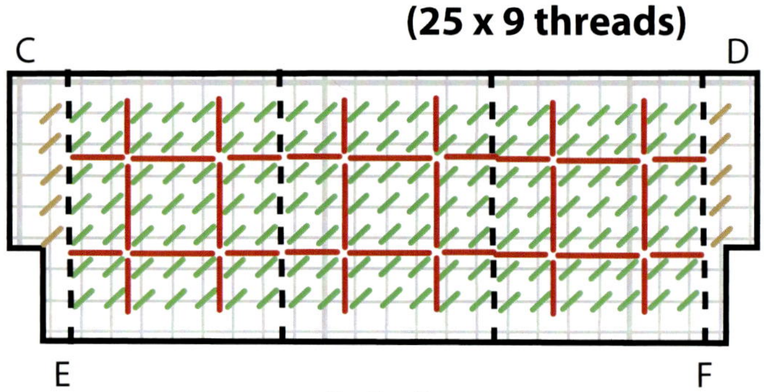

Sofa Front
(25 x 10 threads)

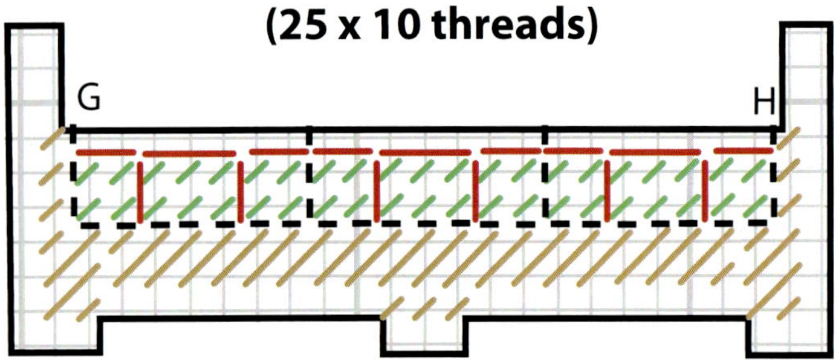

Sofa Seat
(23 x 7 threads)

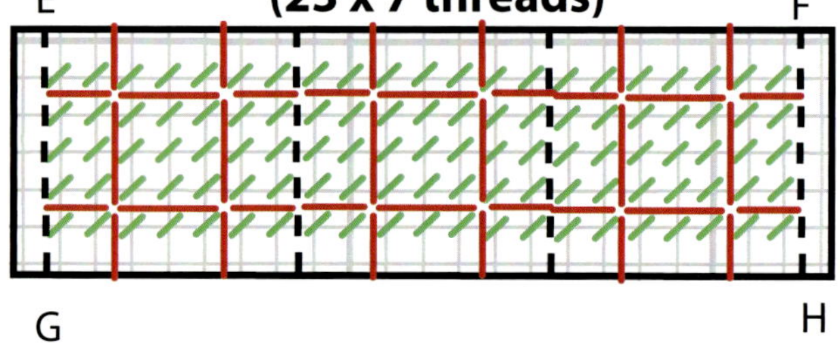

Front of Headboard
(20 x 8 threads)

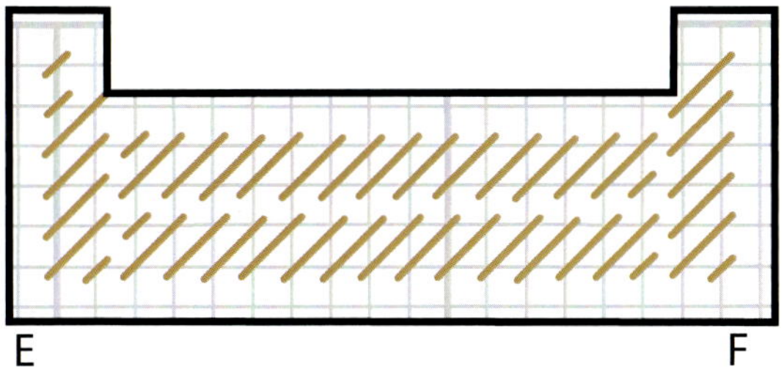

Front of Footboard
(20 x 6 threads)

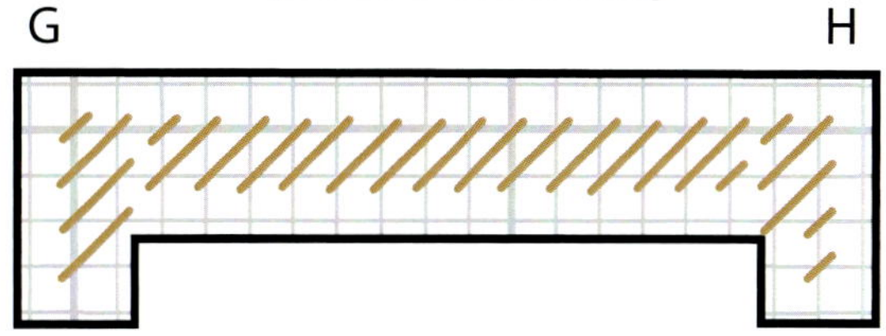

Double Bed Sides
(8 x 30 threads each)

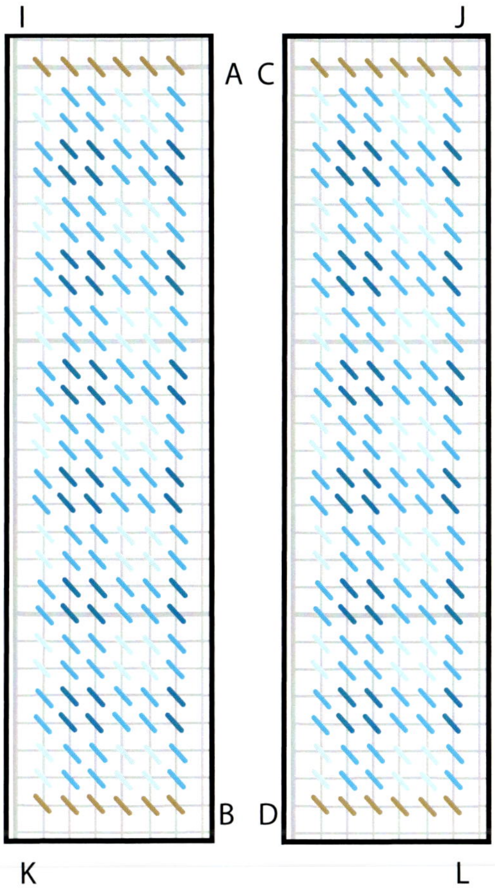

Double Bed Top
(20 x 28 threads)

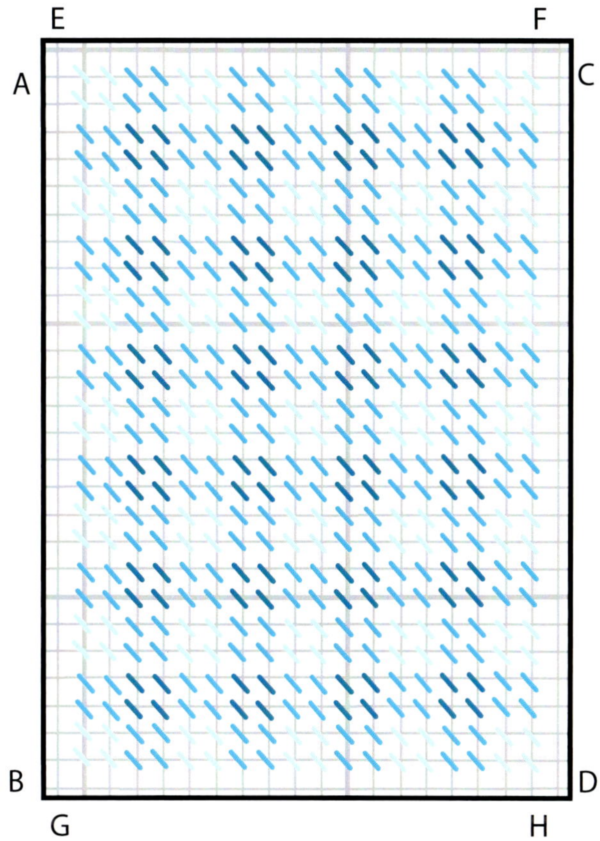

Back of Headboard
(20 x 15 threads)

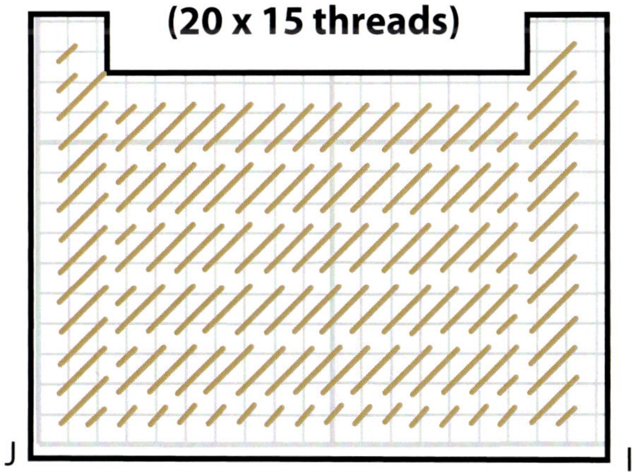

Back of Footboard
(20 x 13 threads)

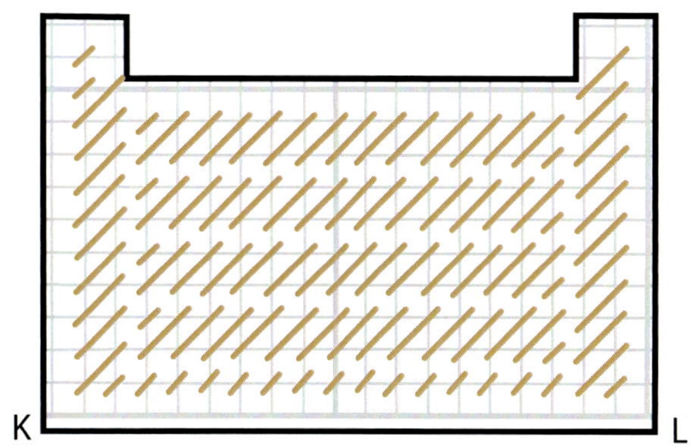

Night Stand Top
(7 x 8 threads)

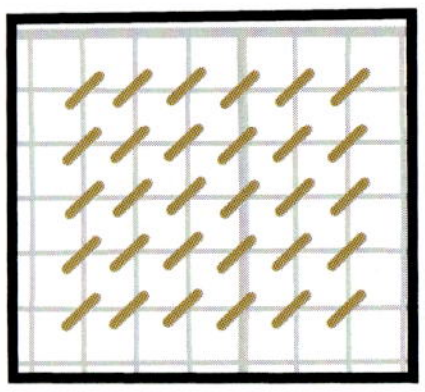

Night Stand Front
(9 x 8 threads)

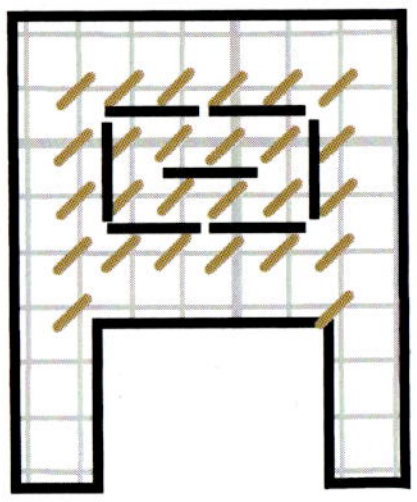

Night Stand Back
(9 x 8 threads)

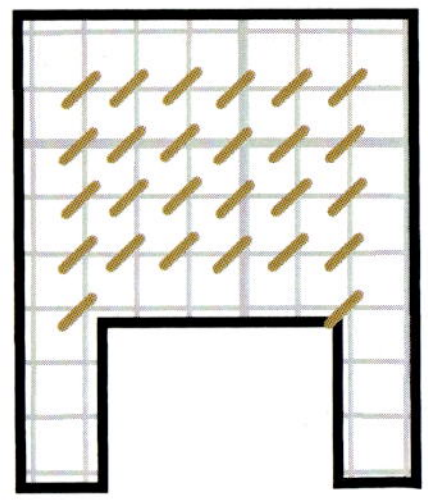

Night Stand Side
(cut 2)
(9 x 7 threads)

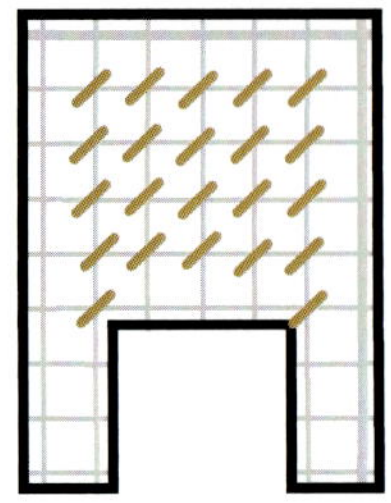

Cedar Chest
Inner End (cut 2)
(7 x 5 threads)

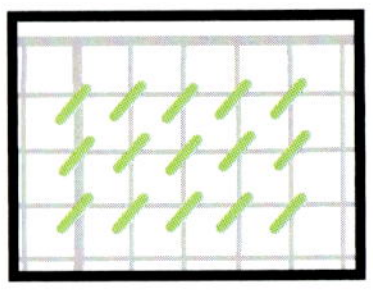

Cedar Chest
Inner Front
(17 x 5 threads)

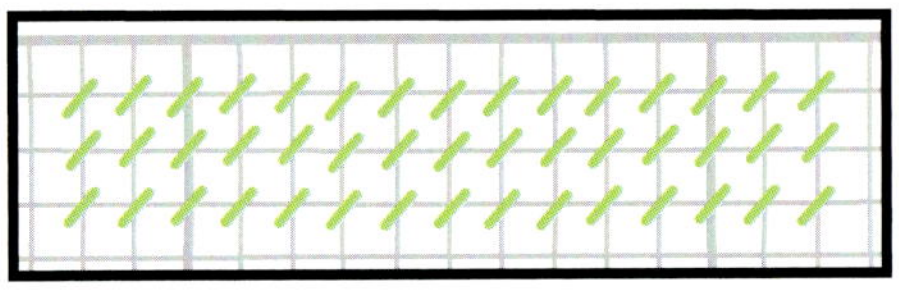

Cedar Chest
Top Edge (cut 2)
(2 x 7 threads)

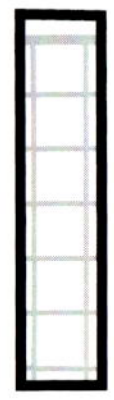

Cedar Chest
Back Edge
(2 x 18 threads)

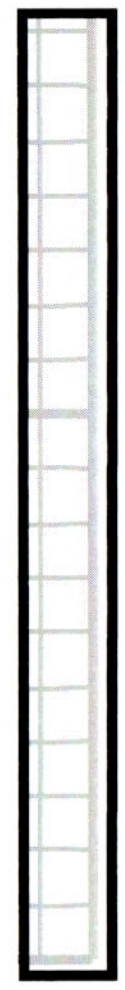

Cedar Chest
Inner Back
(17 x 5 threads)

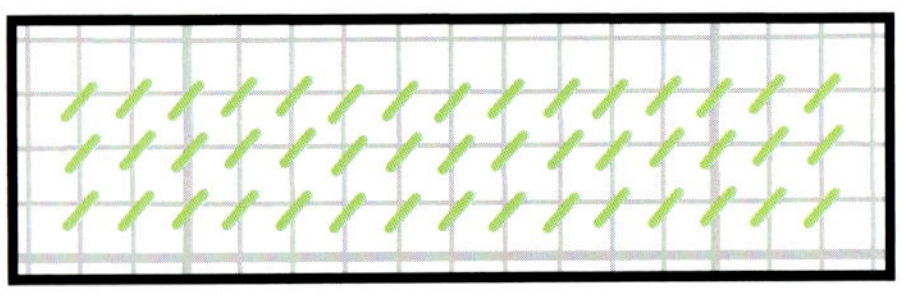

Cedar Chest
Inner Bottom
(17 x 7 threads)

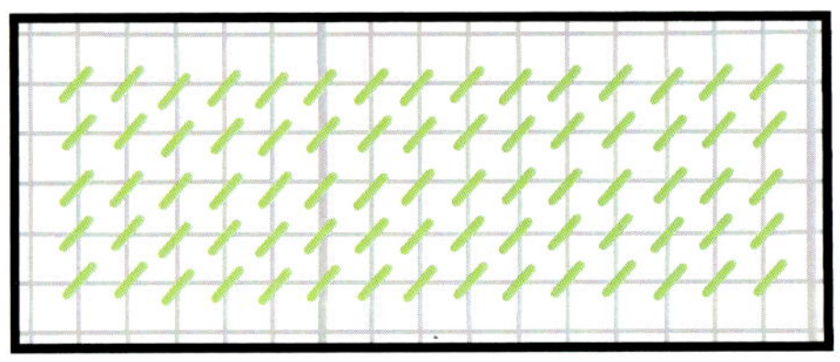

Cedar Chest
Inner Top
(20 x 10 threads)

Cedar Chest
Outer Top
(20 x 10 threads)

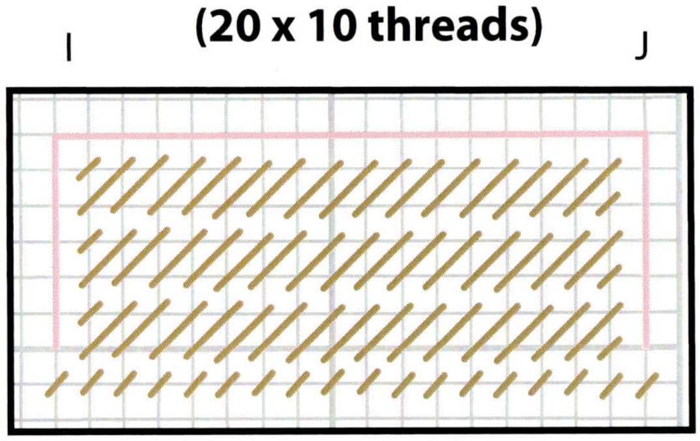

Cedar Chest
Outer Ends
(8 x 6 threads each)

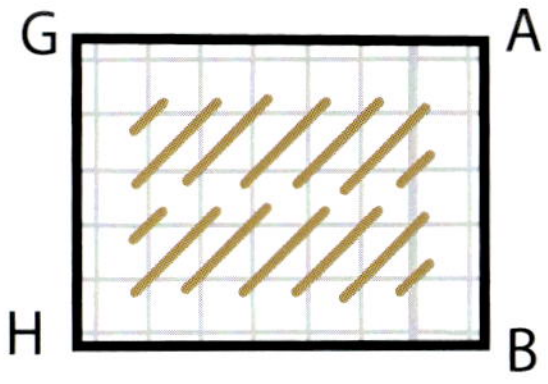

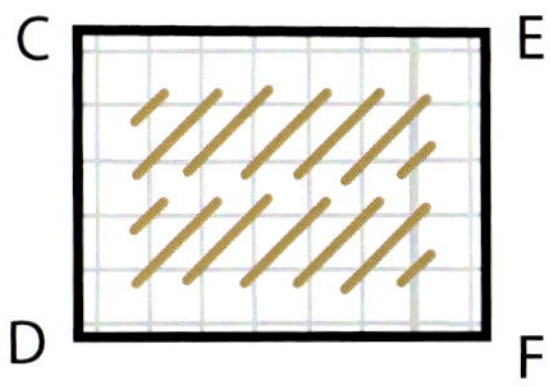

Cedar Chest
Outer Front
(18 x 6 threads)

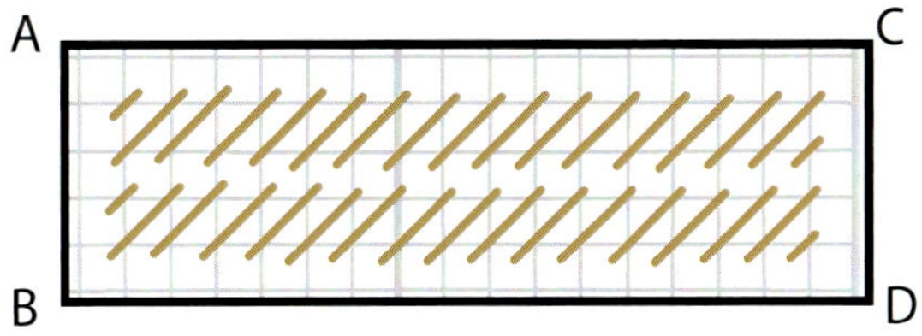

Cedar Chest
Outer Back
(18 x 6 threads)

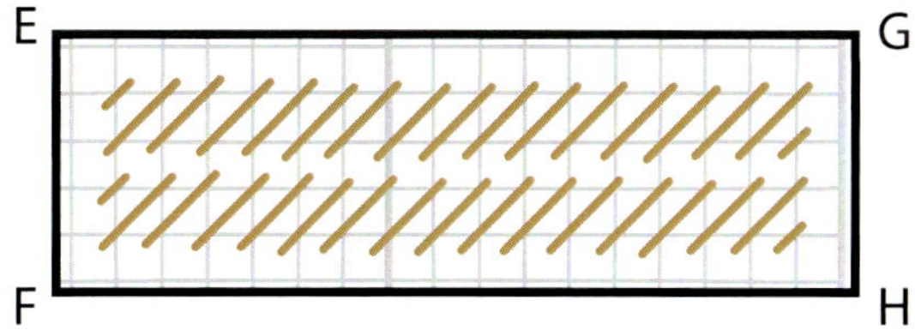

Cedar Chest
Cushion Top
(16 x 7 threads)

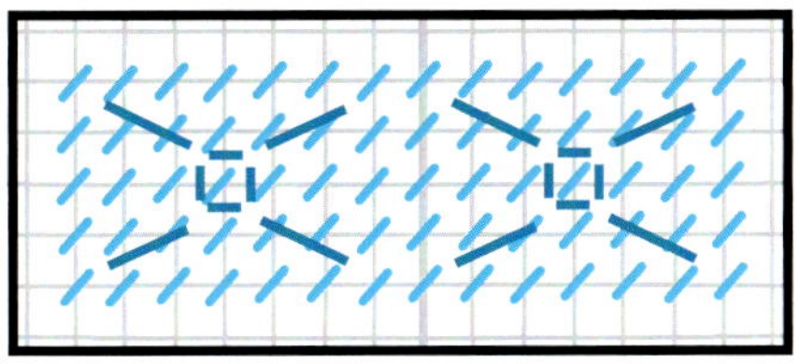

Cedar Chest
Cushion Bottom
(16 x 7 threads)

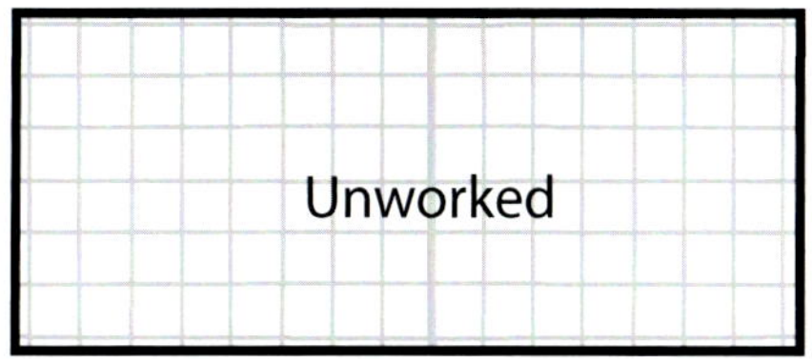

Cedar Chest
Cushion Short Side
(cut 2)
(2 x 7 threads)

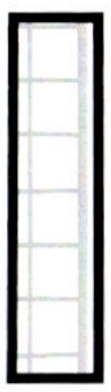

Cedar Chest
Cushion Long Side (cut 2)
(16 x 2 threads)

Dresser Top
(17 x 7 threads)

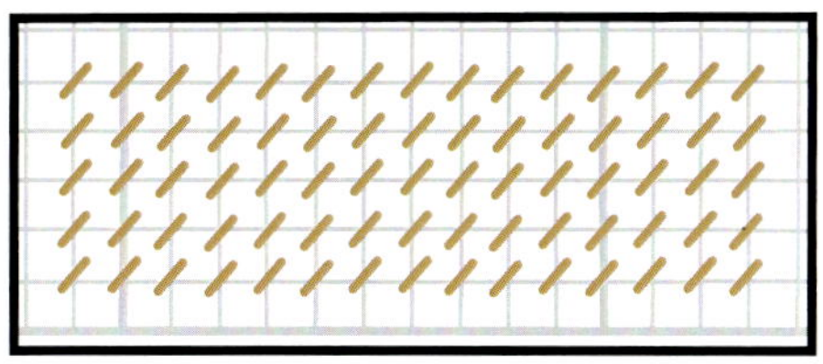

Dresser Back
(17 x 12 threads)

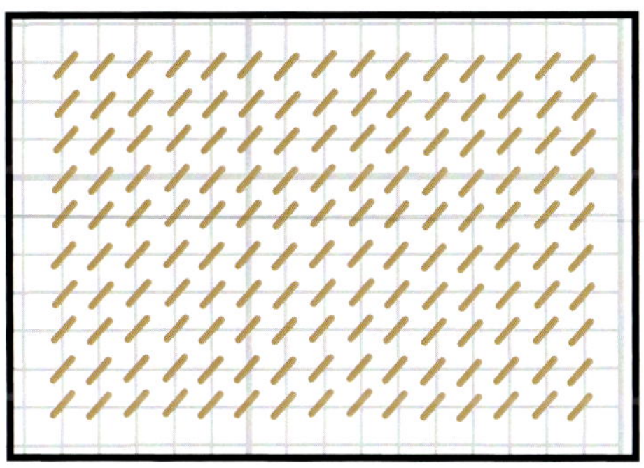

Dresser Side (cut 2)
(7 x 12 threads)

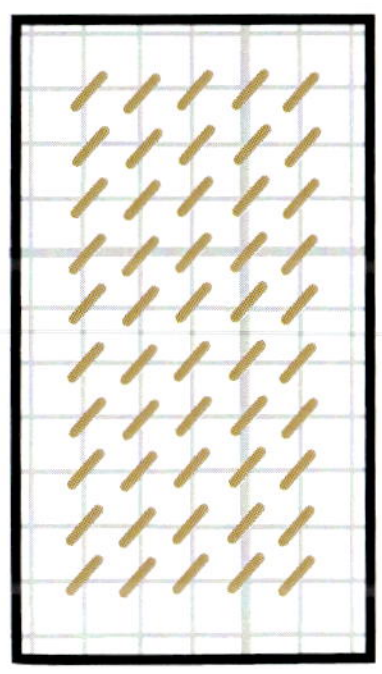

Dresser Front
(17 x 12 threads)

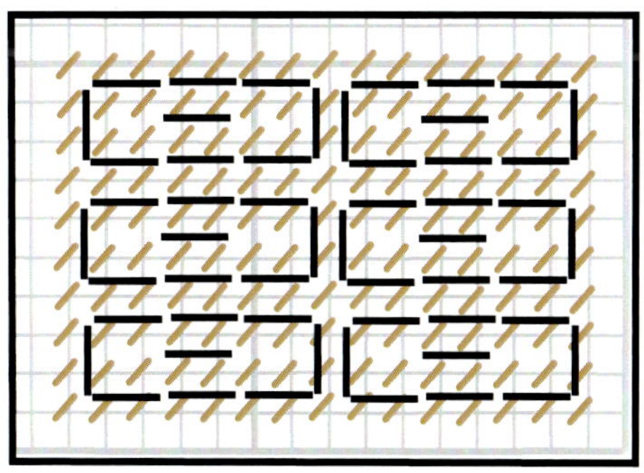

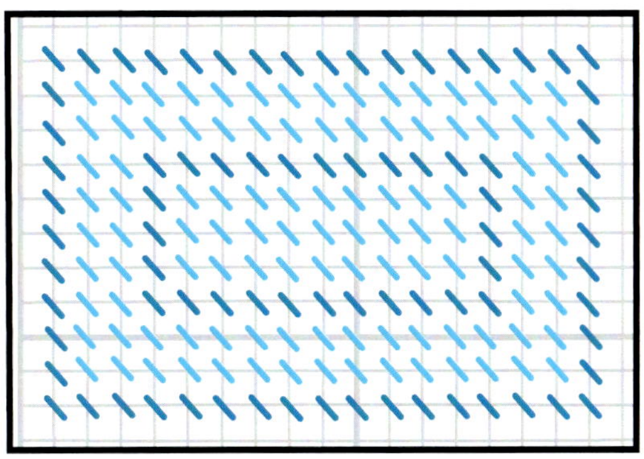

Loft Rug #1
(19 x 13
threads)

Upper Headboard
(12 x 6 threads)

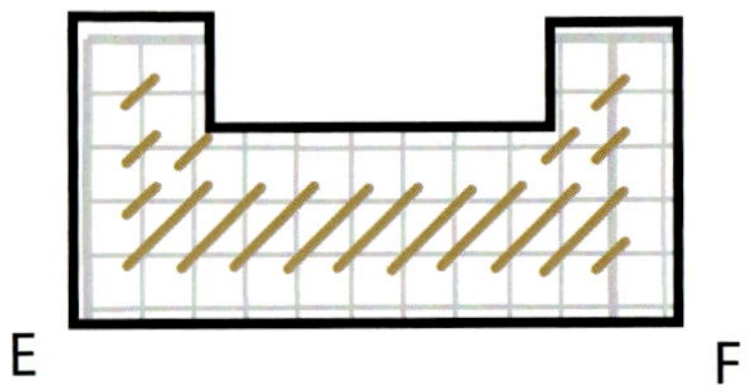

Upper Footboard
(12 x 6 threads)

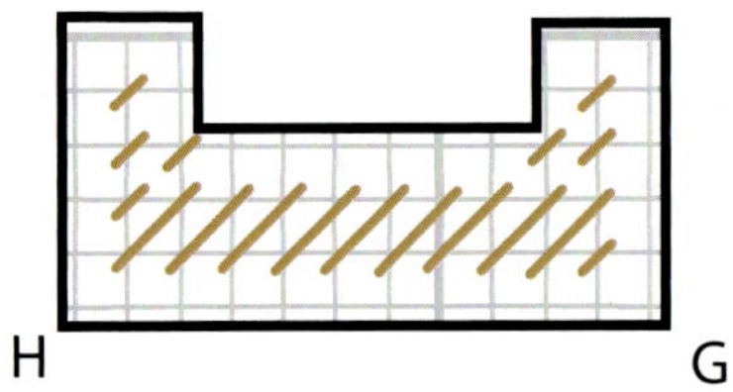

Ladder
(9 x 24 threads)

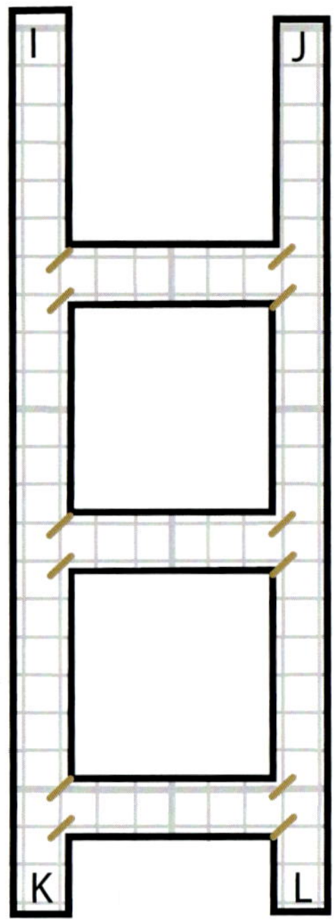

Lower Headboard
(12 x 17 threads)

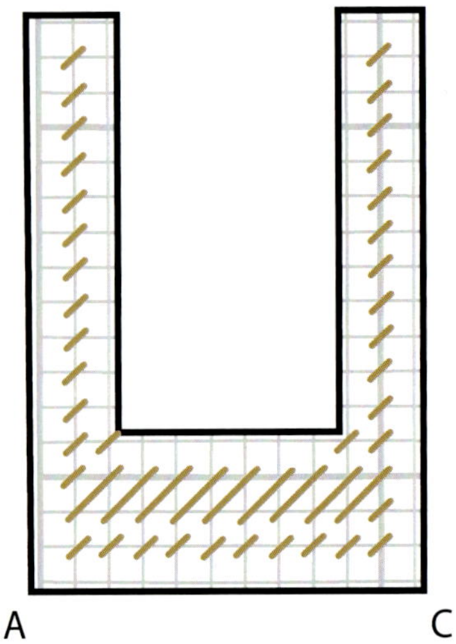

Lower Footboard
(12 x 17 threads)

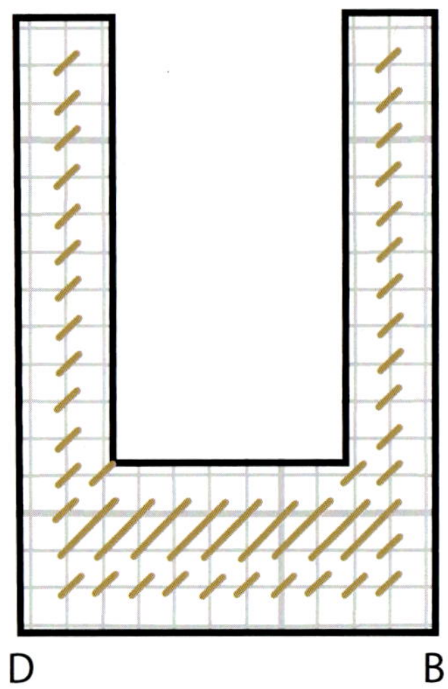

Bunk Tops
(28 x 12 threads)

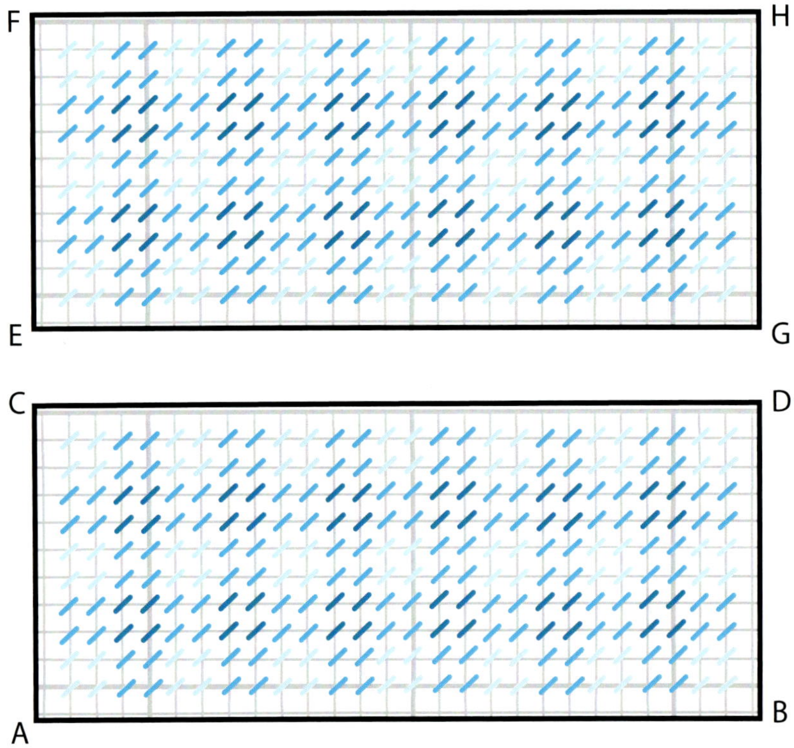

Loft Rug #2
(10 x 28 threads)

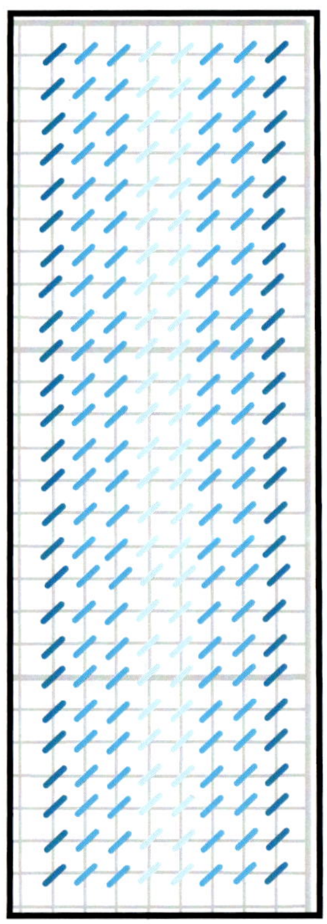

Bunk Bed Front (30 x 34 threads)

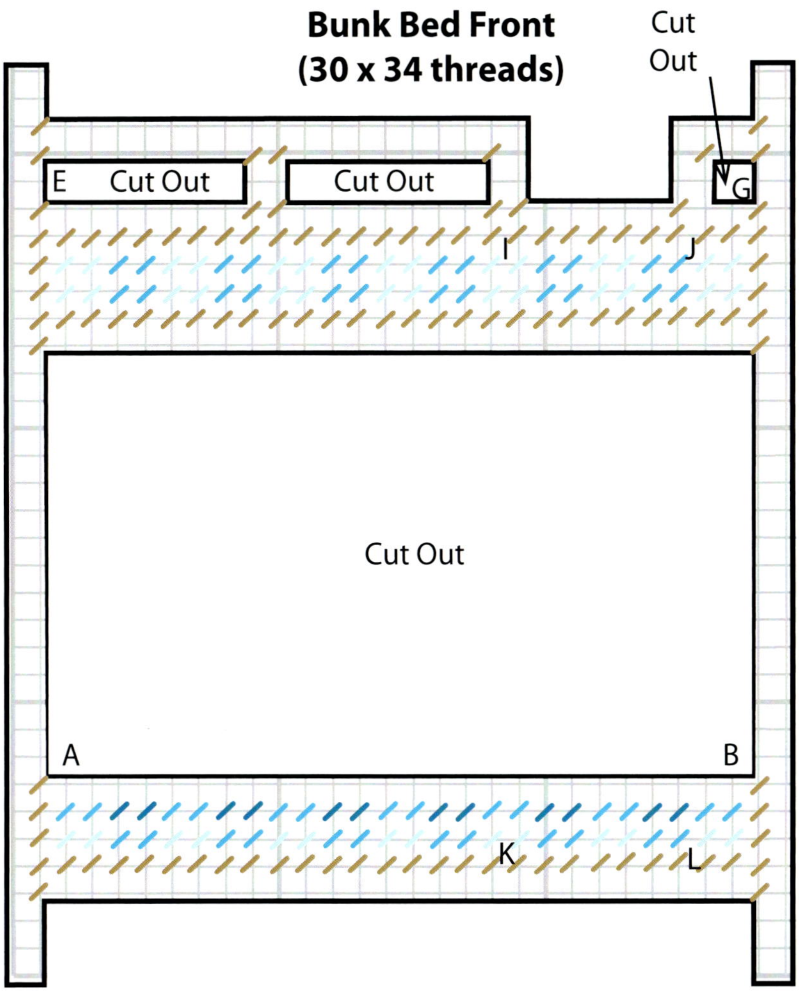

Bunk Bed End (cut 2) **(12 x 34 threads)**

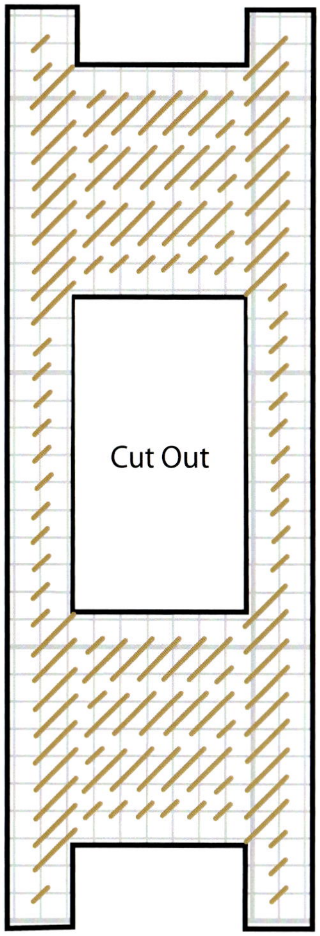

Bunk Bed Back (30 x 34 threads)

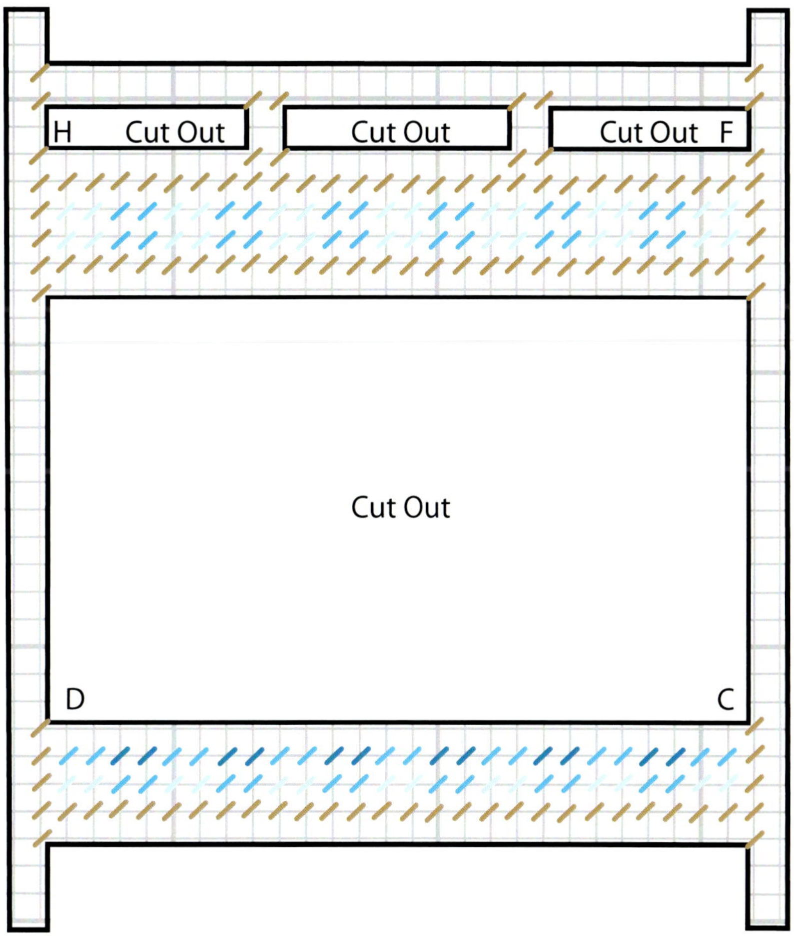

Outhouse Interior Back (18 x 29 threads)

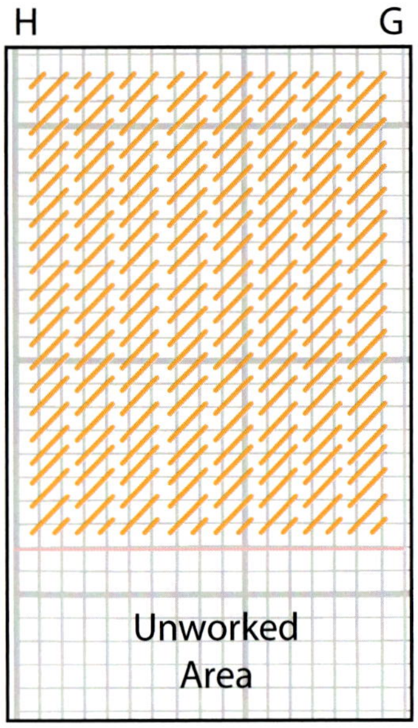

Outhouse Interior Left (22 x 36 threads)

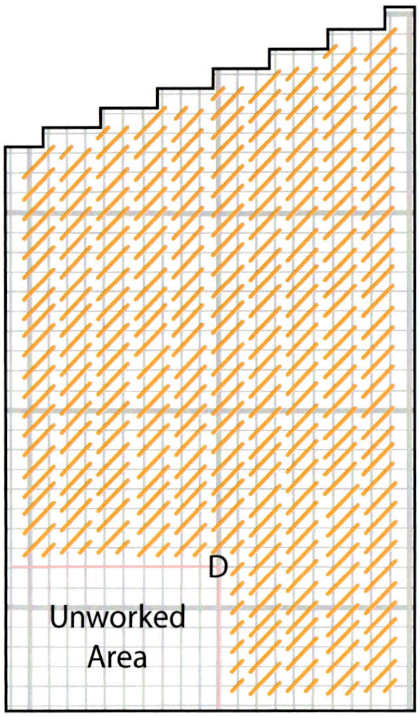

Outhouse Interior Front (18 x 36 threads)

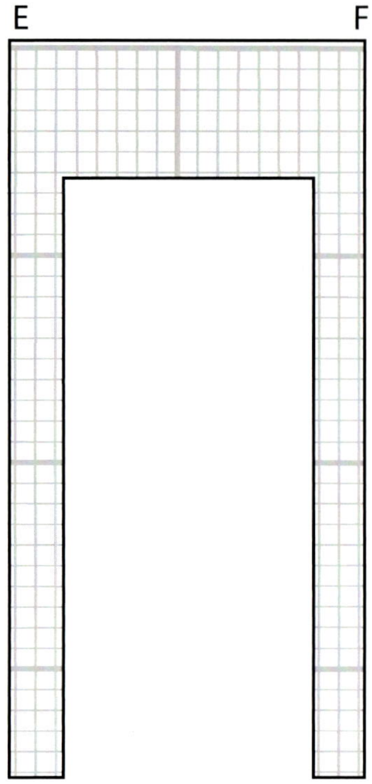

Outhouse Interior Right (22 x 36 threads)

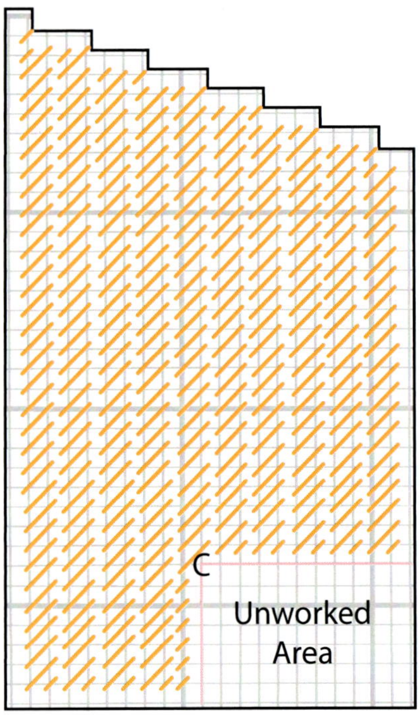

Outhouse Front Door (14 x 31 threads)

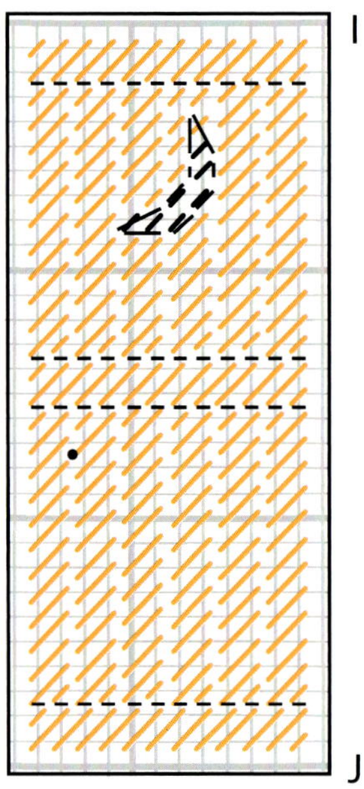

Outhouse Back Door (14 x 31 threads)

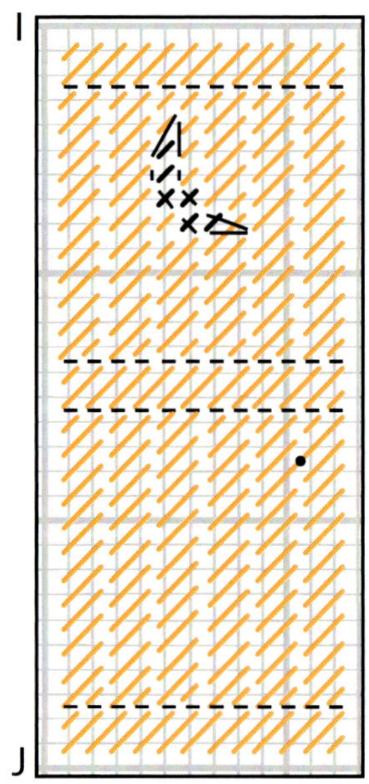

Outhouse Exterior Back (20 x 30 threads)

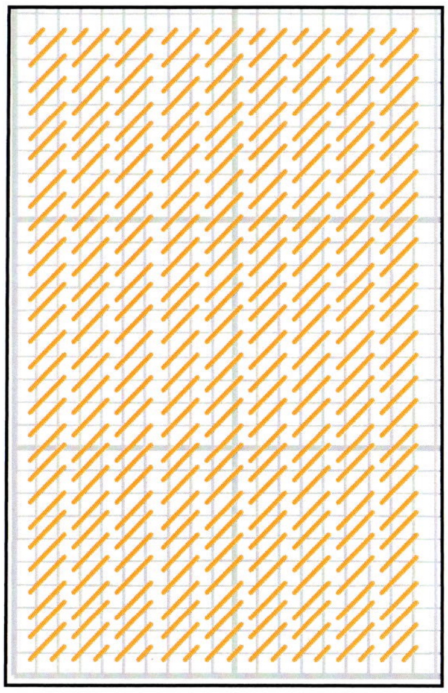

Outhouse Exterior Left (24 x 37 threads)

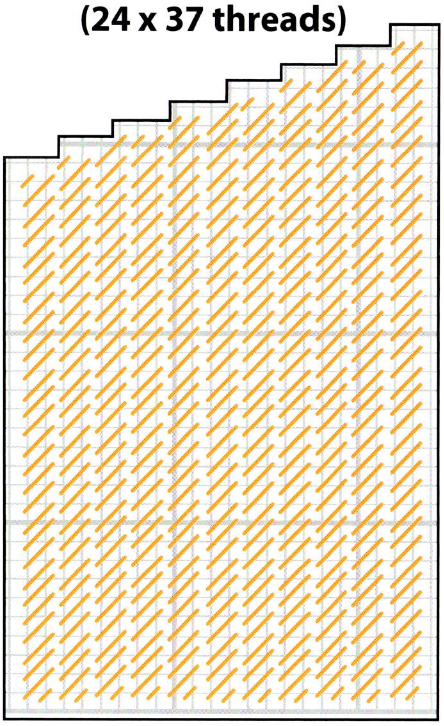

Outhouse Exterior Front (20 x 37 threads)

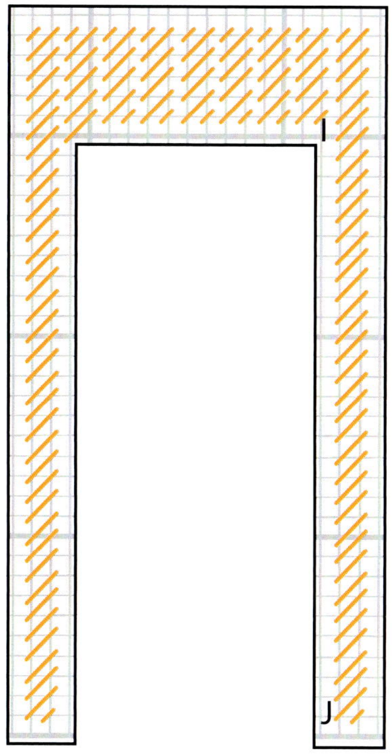

Outhouse Exterior Right (24 x 37 threads)

Outhouse Roof (24 x 30 threads)

Outhouse Roof Underside (24 x 30 threads)

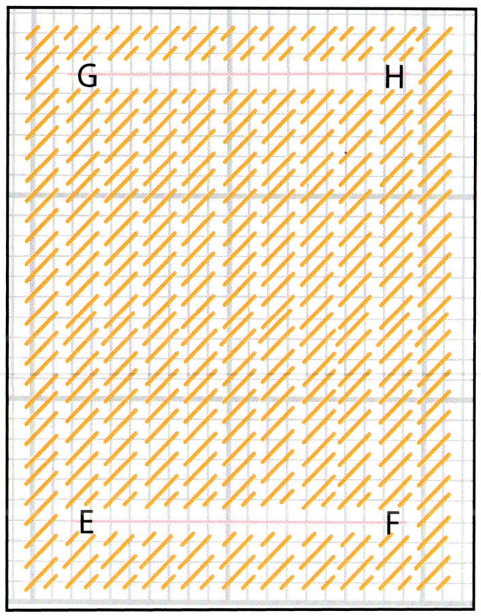

Outhouse Seat Lid (8 x 10 threads)

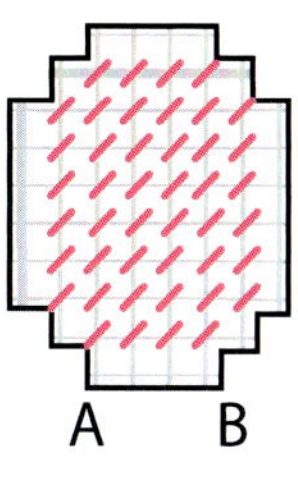

Outhouse Seat (8 x 10 threads)

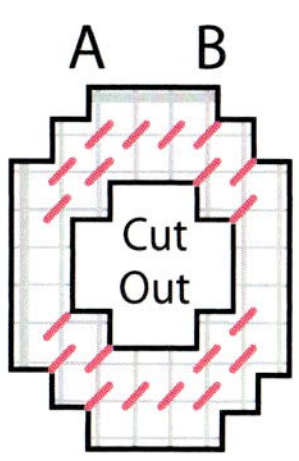

Double Chair Back
(22 x 16 threads)

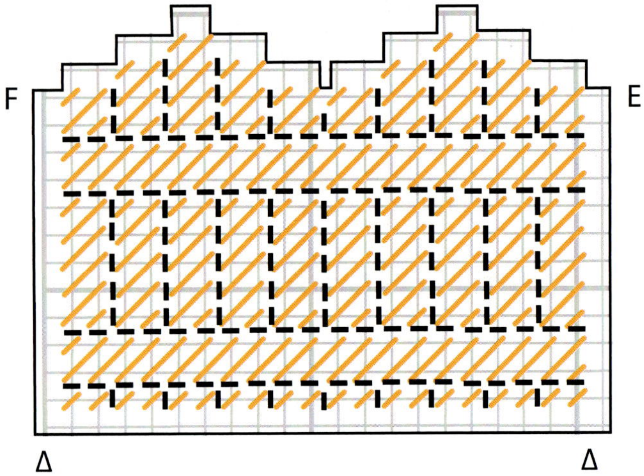

Double Chair Front
(22 x 16 threads)

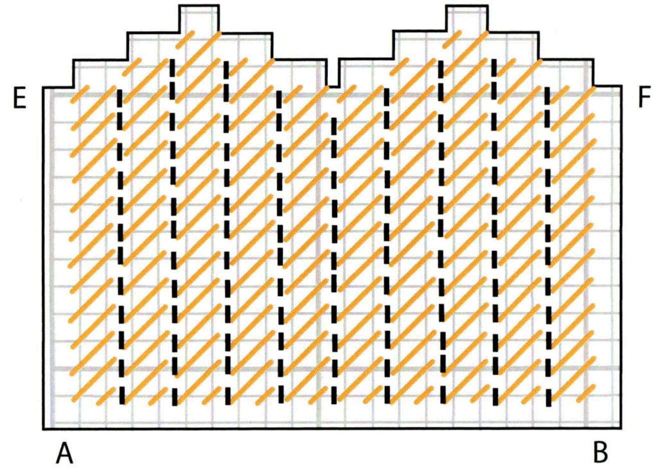

Double Chair Seat
(22 x 12 threads)

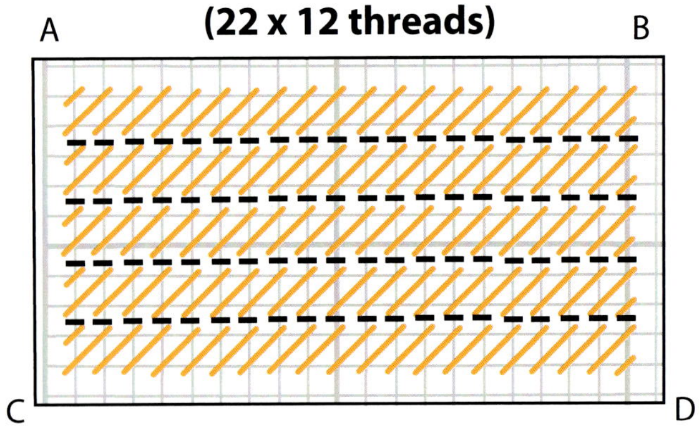

Outhouse Base
(34 x 38 threads)

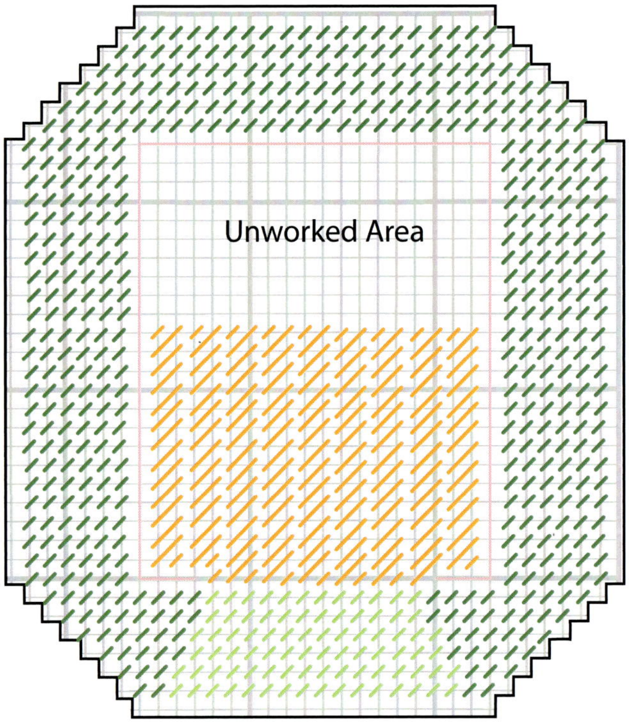

Outhouse Bench Top
(18 x 12 threads)

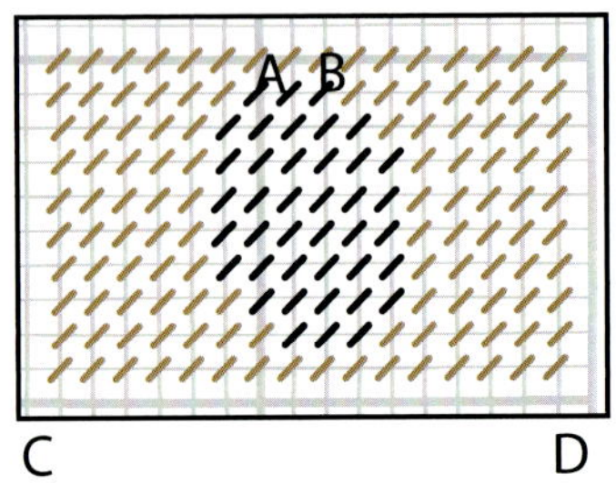

Outhouse Bench Front
(18 x 8 threads)

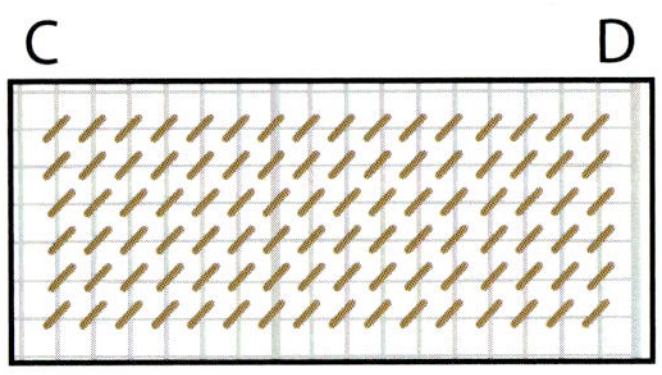

Chair Arm Bottom
(cut 6)
(9 x 2 threads)

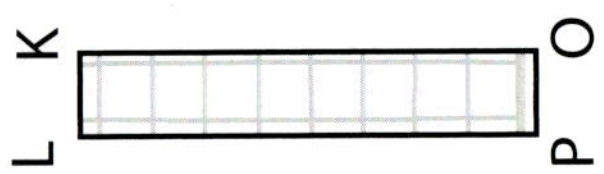

Chair Arm Back
(cut 6)
(10 x 2 threads)

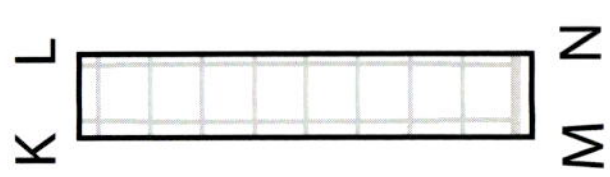

Chair Arm Front
(cut 6)
(12 x 2 threads)

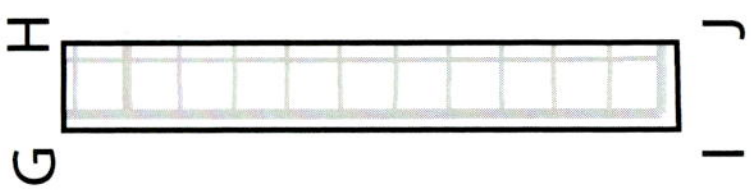

Chair Inner Right Side
(cut 3) **(18 x 17 threads)**

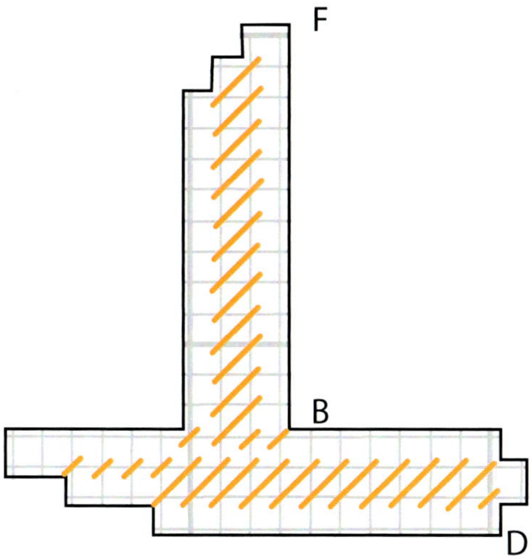

Chair Outer Right Side
(cut 3) **(18 x 17 threads)**

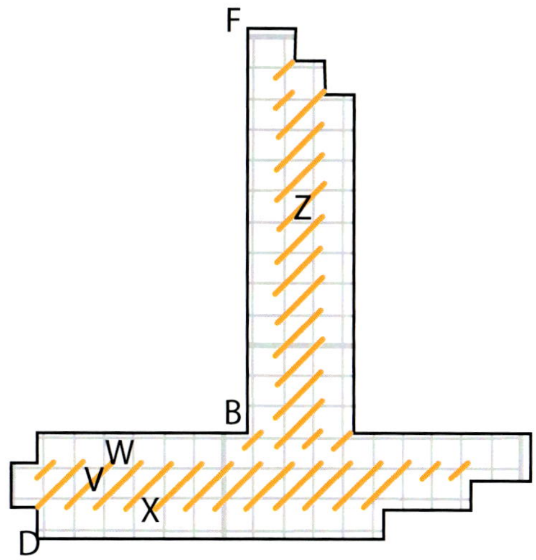

Picnic Table Bench Undersides
(6 x 31 threads each)

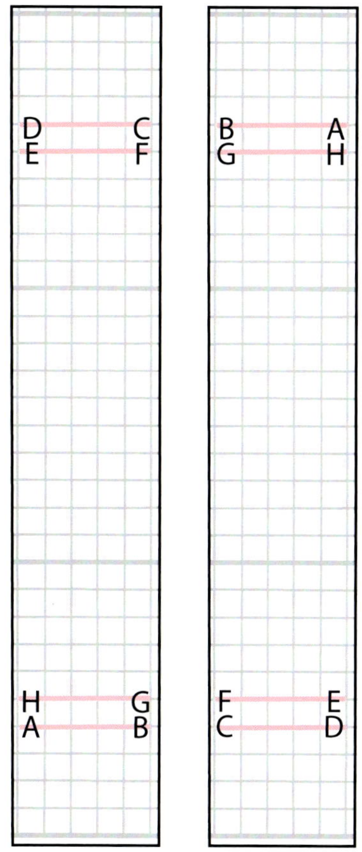

Chair Outer Left Side (cut 3)
(18 x 17 threads)

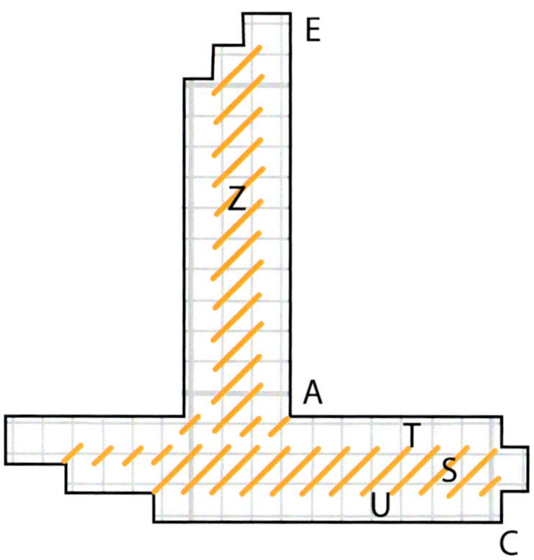

Chair Inner Left Side (cut 3)
(18 x 17 threads)

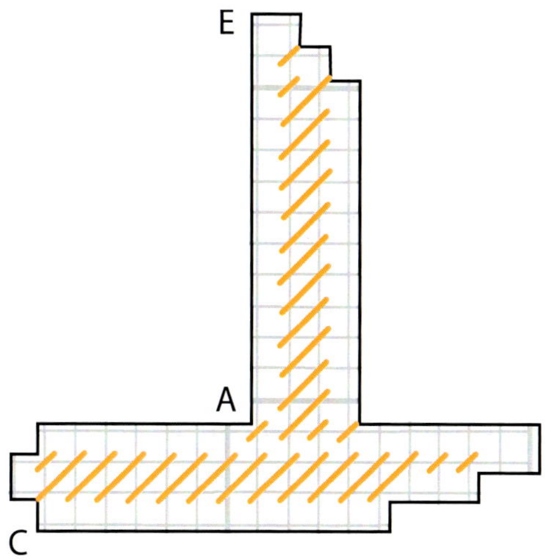

Picnic Table Left Leg
(cut 2)
(4 x 15 threads)

Picnic Table Right Leg
(cut 2)
(4 x 15 threads)

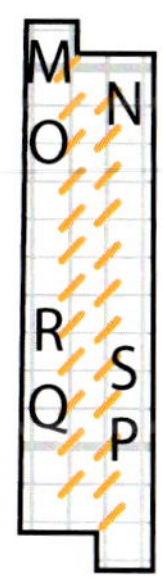

Picnic Table Cross Bars (cut 2 each)
(27 x 4 threads each)

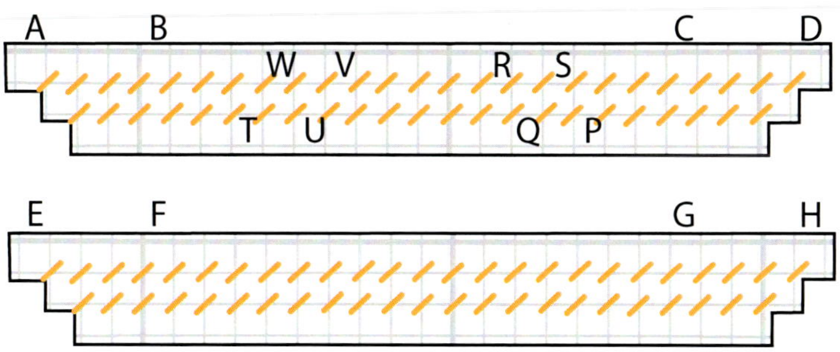

Picnic Table Bench Top (cut 2)
(31 x 6 threads)

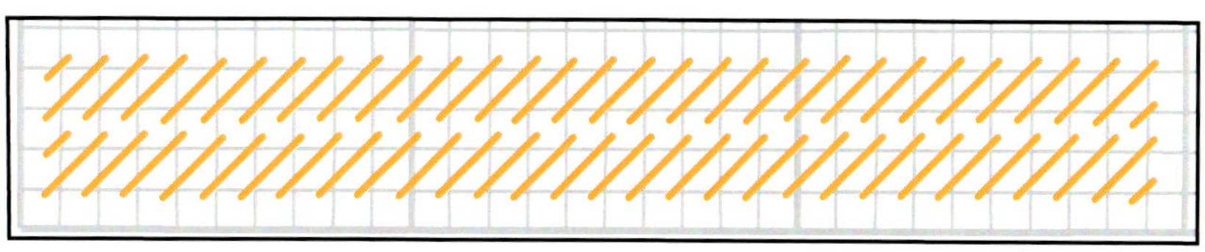

Chair Outer Left Arm
(cut 3) **(13 x 12 threads)**

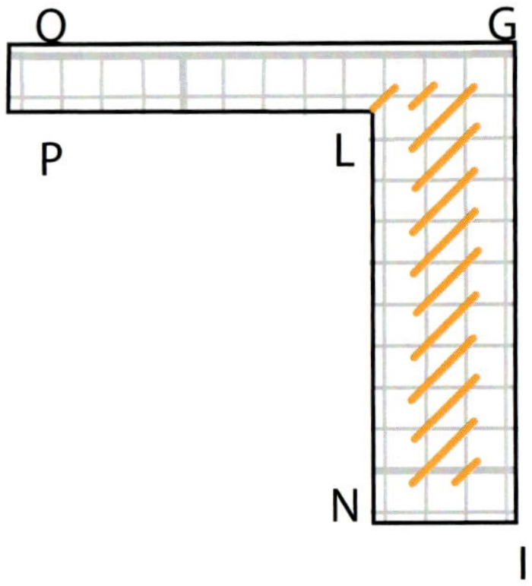

Chair Inner Left Arm
(cut 3) **(13 x 12 threads)**

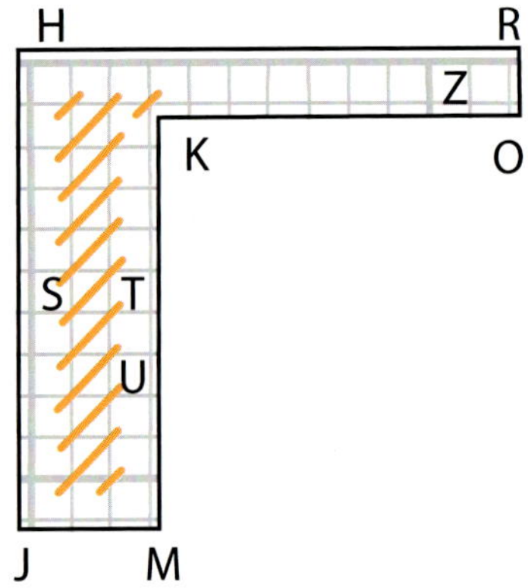

Picnic Table Support Blocks (6 x 4 threads)

Chair Inner Right Arm
(cut 3) **(13 x 12 threads)**

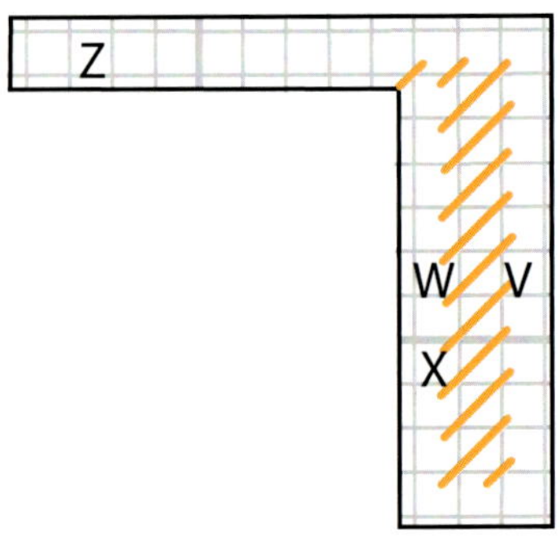

Chair Outer Right Arm
(cut 3) **(13 x 12 threads)**

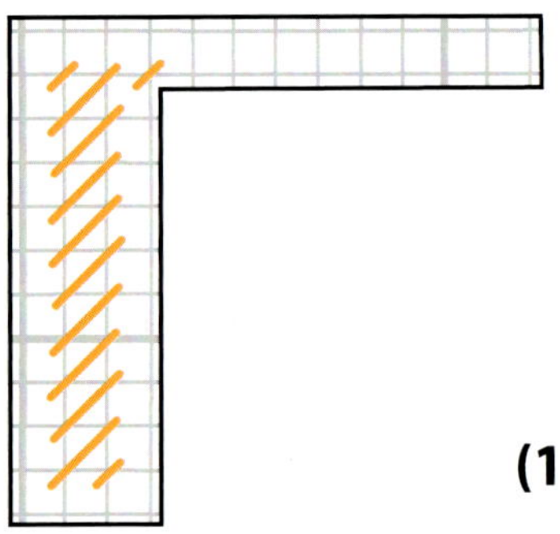

Picnic Table Underside (12 x 31 threads)

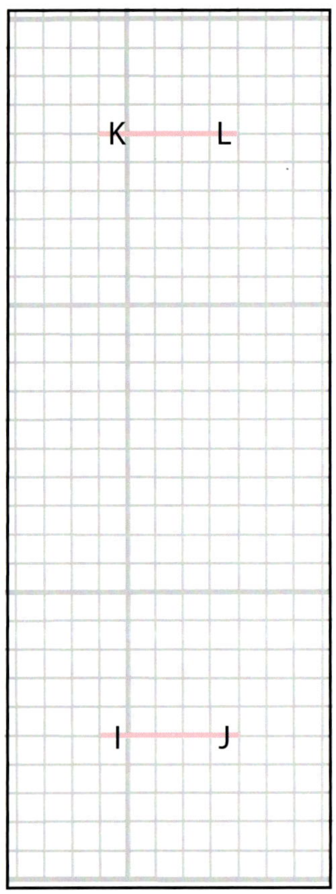

Picnic Table Top (12 x 31 threads)

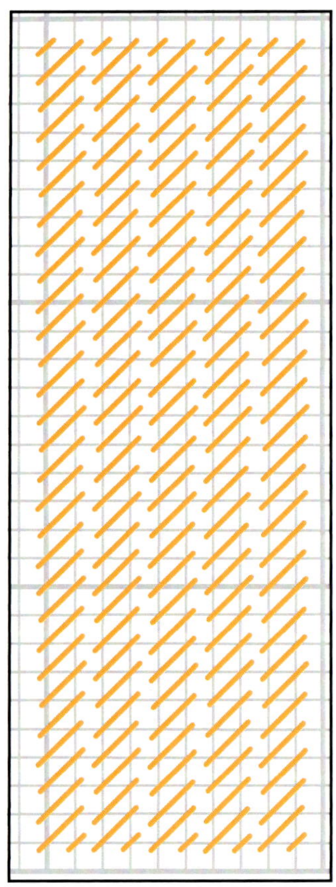

Chair Left Arm Top (cut 3)
(14 x 4 threads)

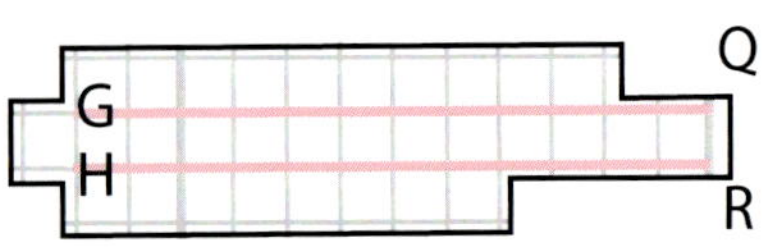

Chair Right Arm Top (cut 3)
(14 x 4 threads)

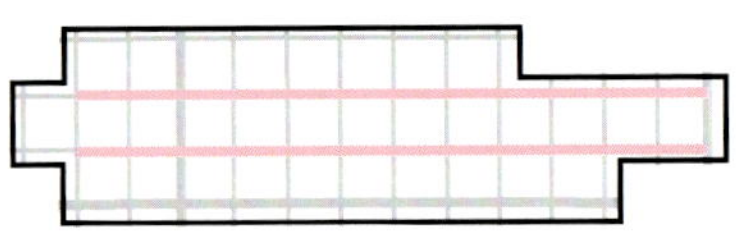

Chair Back
(cut 2)
(12 x 16 threads)

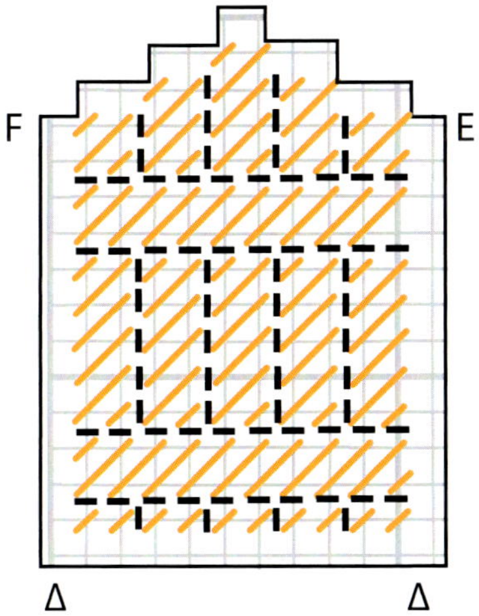

Chair Front
(cut 2)
(12 x 16 threads)

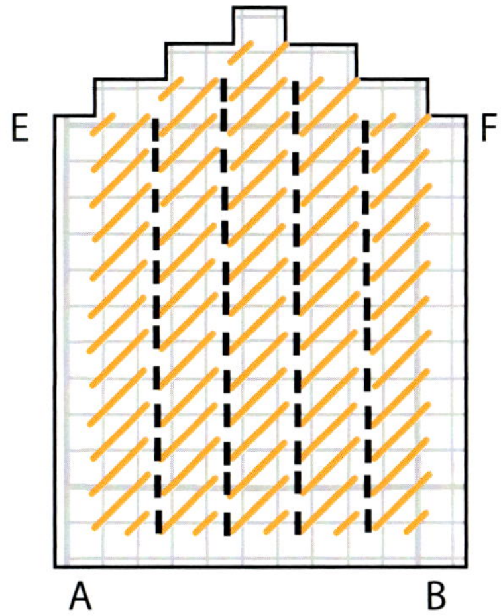

Chair Seat
(cut 2)
(12 x 12 threads)

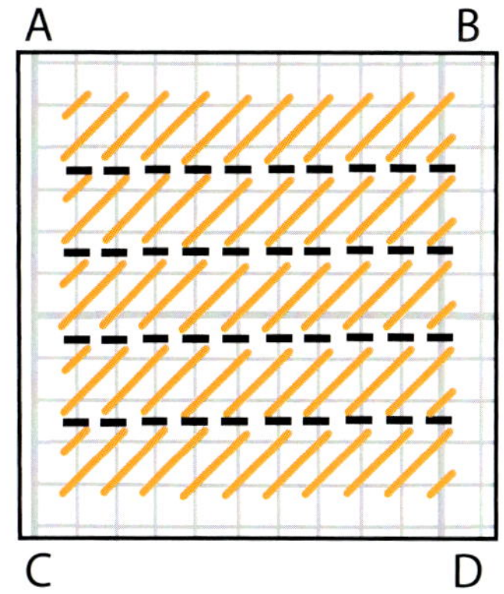

Campfire Top
(38 x 38 threads)

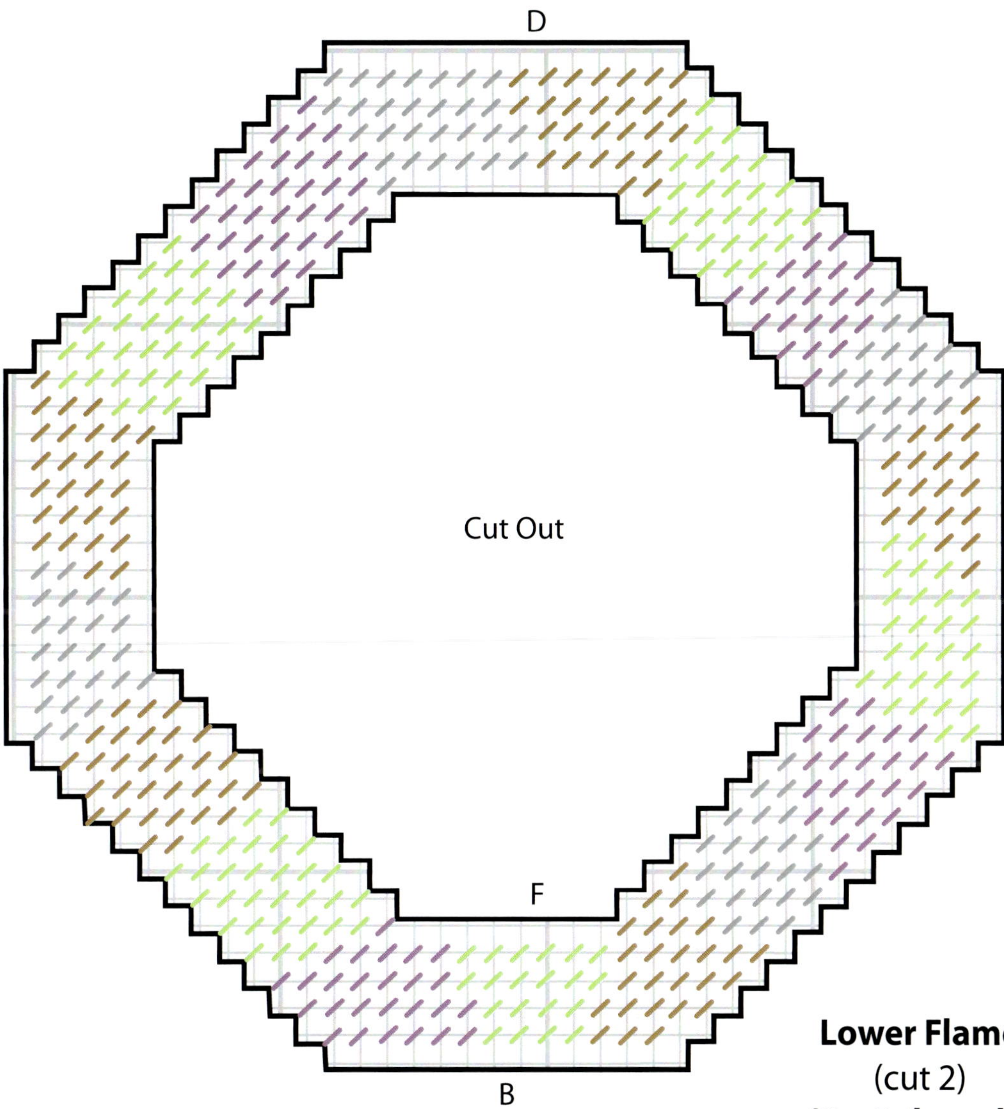

Long Bark (cut 4)
(13 x 8 threads)

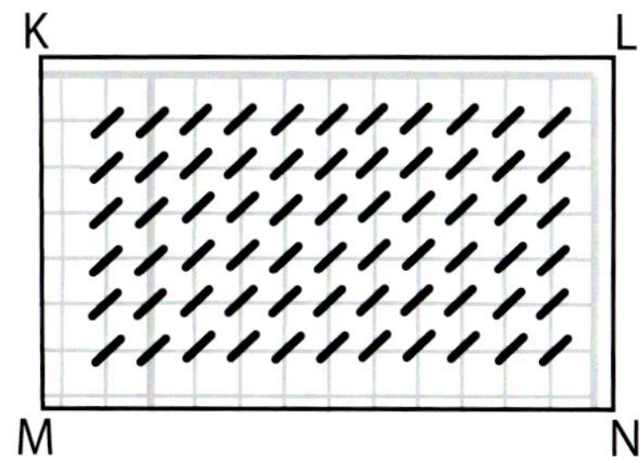

Short Bark (cut 2)
(4 x 8 threads)

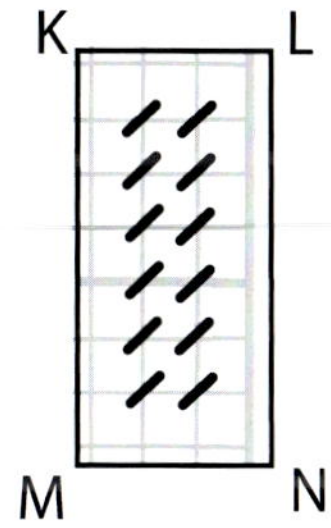

Lower Flame →
(cut 2)
(6 x 8 threads)

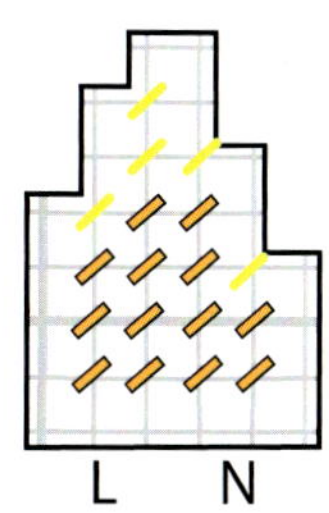

Campfire Base
(38 x 38 threads)

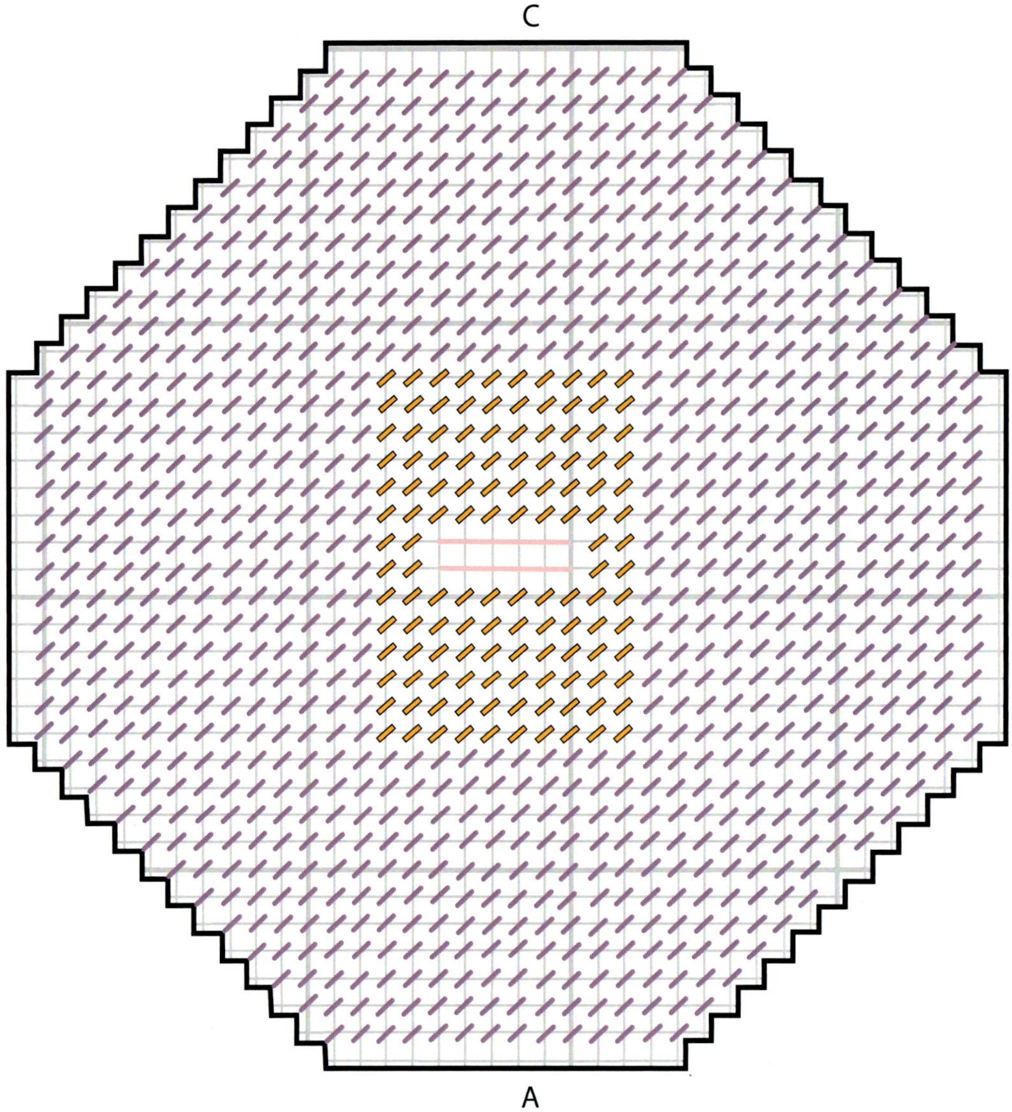

Log End (cut 10)
(3 x 4 threads)

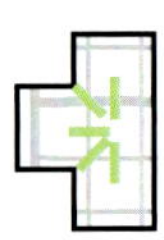

Long Log (cut 4)
(13 x 4 threads)

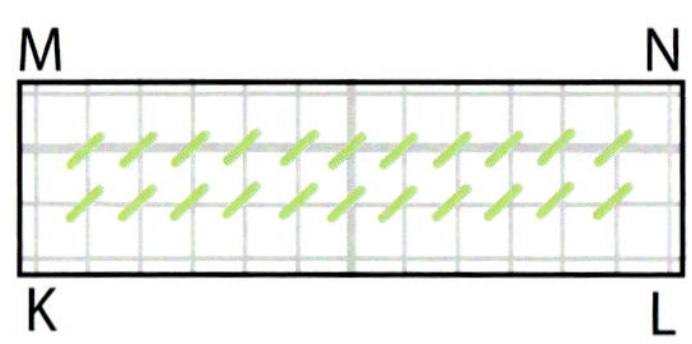

Short Log (cut 2)
(4 x 4 threads)

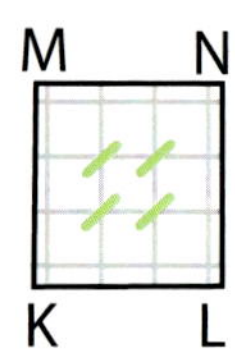

Center Flames
(11 x 9 threads each)

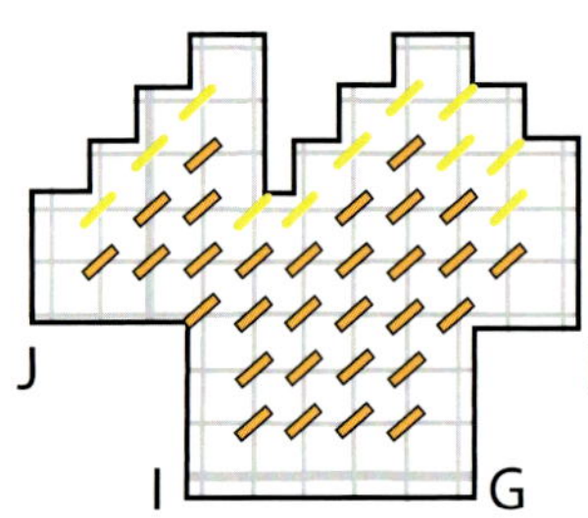

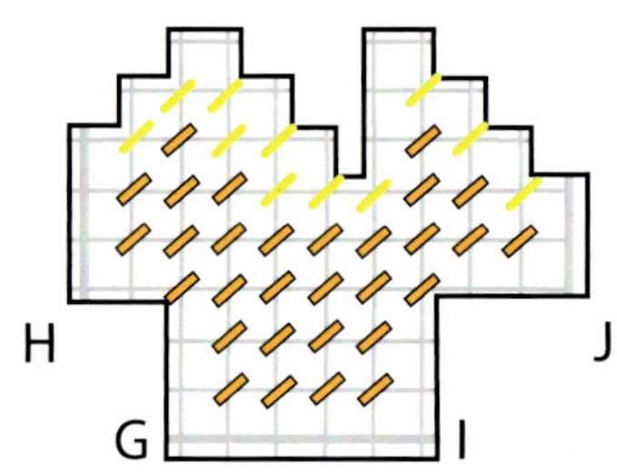

Campfire Outer Side I
(61 x 5 threads)

Campfire Outer Side II
(62 x 5 threads)

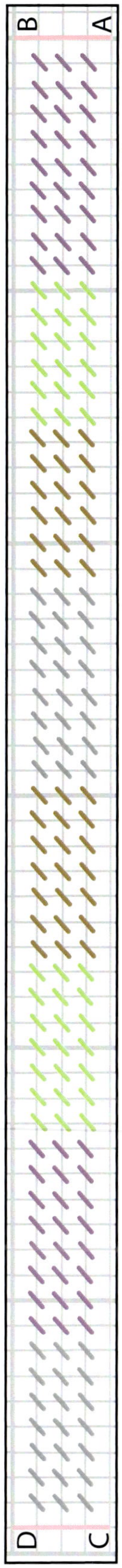

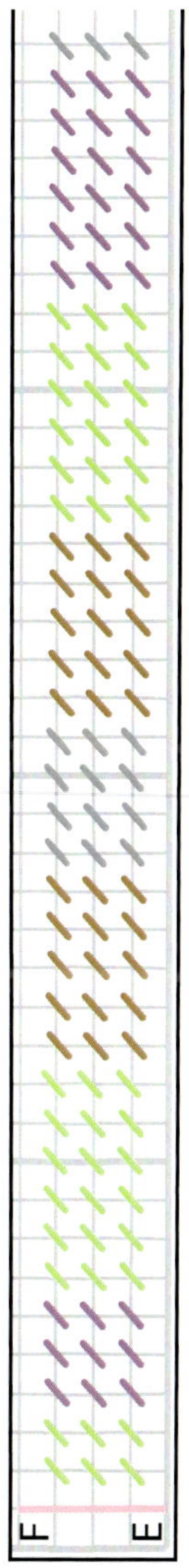

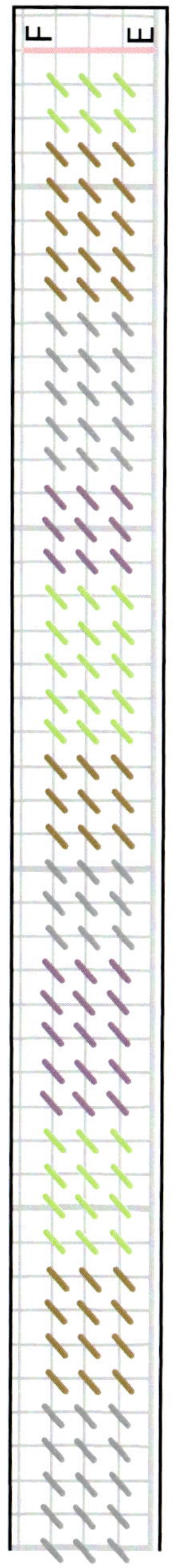

Campfire Inner Side (86 x 5 threads)

This Inner Side chart represents one 86 x 5 thread canvas piece. It is divided into two sections to make it large enough to be followed easily. No threads or stitches are repeated from one piece to the next.

General Instructions

NOTE:

Please read all of the instructions before beginning. When joining pieces, refer to photos and notice whether right side of stitching should face in or out. You may need to use a few common household items to complete your project.

GENERAL INSTRUCTIONS:

Cutting the canvas must be done very carefully. If you miscut, the piece is ruined and you'll have to cut another piece. Our graphs show the shape of the pieces when they are cut out, making it easier for you to follow the cutting line. To cut, count threads, not holes. On each graph we show the total maximum number of threads required for each piece. (If you find it necessary to mark on canvas, use a pencil, but use it cautiously as the yarn will pick up the marks.) Plastic canvas is hand washable but do not put it in the dryer and do not dry clean. Cut in the space between the threads (as shown on the graph) rather than on a thread. After cutting, you will need to trim off all plastic nubs that remain to give your work a more finished look.

STITCHING INSTRUCTIONS:

Using 1 yard pieces of yarn, keep an even tension, making sure canvas is completely covered. However, too tight a tension will cause the canvas to curl. Work row across, first from left to right, then returning from right to left. To begin strand, draw needle through canvas until about 1/2" [1 cm] remains at back. Hold this end close to canvas and catch it in stitches on reverse side of work. To end each strand, put needle through to back and draw under a few stitches to secure. Trim yarn close to work. Start overcast stitches in the middle of rows where possible, instead of the corners. This will make the corners stronger. All joining rows and indicated areas are unworked.

Stitches

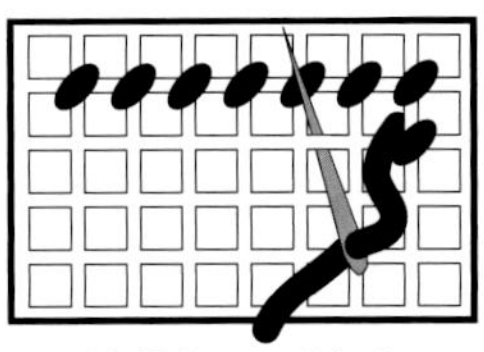

Half Cross Stitch

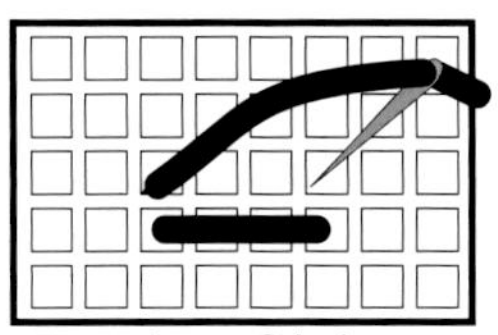

Long Stitch

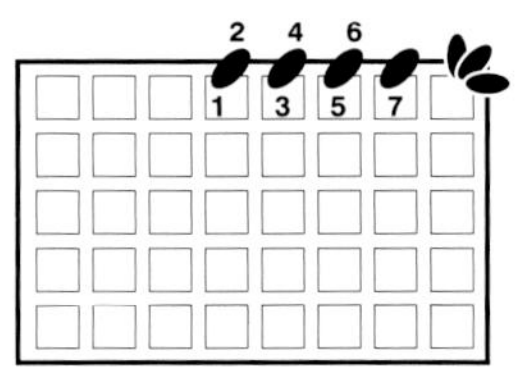

Overcast Stitch

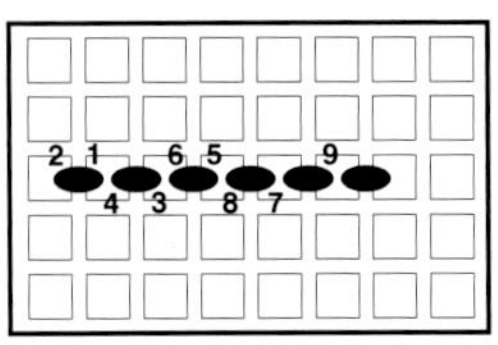

Backstitch

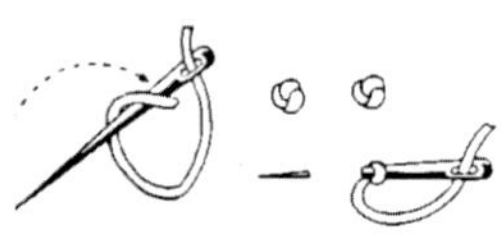

French Knot

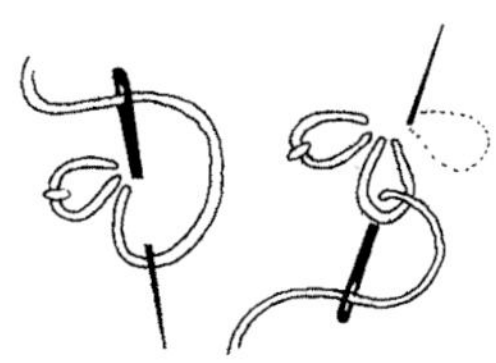

Lazy Daisy

Made in U.S.A.